NEW TECHNOLOGIES
IN THE ARTROOM

DEBORAH GREH

A Handbook for Teachers
Updated Edition

NEW TECHNOLOGIES IN THE ARTROOM

DEBORAH GREH

A Handbook for Teachers

DAVIS PUBLICATIONS, INC.

Worcester, Massachusetts • www.davis-art.com

To Colleen

New Technologies in the Artroom
Updated Edition

Publisher: Wyatt Wade
Editorial Director: Helen Ronan
Production Editor: Carol Harley
Manufacturing Coordinator: Jenna Sturgis
Editorial Assistance: Colleen Strang
Copyeditors: Lynn Simon, Janet Stone
Design: Jeannet Leendertse

Library of Congress Catalog Card Number: 2002111213
ISBN: 87192-611-3
10 9 8 7 6 5 4 3 2 1
Printed in the United States of America

Cover, top to bottom: Art Isom,
Justin Tugya, Leroy Jones, Hendrick
Müller-Waack.
Frontispiece, top to bottom:
Deborah Hurwitz, Jen Yoo, Nicole
Mangione.
Contents: Andrew Marsh, Justin
Cole, Marissa Ehrenkrantz, Aaron
Pecoraro.
Part One opener: Hendrick Müller-
Waack.
Part Two opener: Ben Wellman
Part Three opener: Lauren Oxer
Part Four opener: Dana Mistretta
Part Five opener: Jenna Schneider
Part Six opener: Henry Myers
Part Seven opener: Marissa
Ehrenkrantz
Part Eight opener: Paul Cleckner

ACKNOWLEDGMENTS

Thanks go to all the art teachers who so graciously sent their students' works for inclusion in this book, and to the many students who allowed their work to be sent! The teachers include:

Shirley Cadmus, George Washington High School, Danville, VA; Jim Carrico, Wright Elementary, Des Moines, IO; Barbara Delikaris, F. M. Gaudineer Middle School Visual Arts Digital Imaging Lab, Springfield, NJ; Mary Eigel, Union High School, Union, MO; Susan Grossberg, Franklin Avenue Middle School, Franklin Lakes, NJ; Kathy Hawk, Lincoln School, Kingsport, TN; Bob Husth, Warnsdorfer School, East Brunswick, NJ; Lorelei Jones, Homewood-Flossmoor High School, Flossmoor, IL; Jim King, Randolph High School, Morristown, NJ; Nancy Knutsen, Triangle School, Hillsborough, NJ; Cathy McGettigan, Tokeneke School, Darien, CT; Gene Niglia, High Mountain Road School, Franklin Lakes, NJ; Nancy Norwood, Arts High School at the Minnesota Center for Arts Education, Golden Valley, MN; Sue Palfrey, Falmouth Middle School, Falmouth, ME; Jane Rawley, Greenfield Elementary, Richmond, VA; Faye Scannell, Medina Elementary School, Bellevue, WA; Anna Ursyn, University of Northern Colorado, Greeley, CO; Kathy Vaughn, Hutchison Elementary School, Herndon, VA; Debi West, Sugar Hill Elementary, Cumming, GA

Thanks to my many friends with the Art Educators of New Jersey including: Phyllis Annett, Diane Fogler, Tony Migliaccio, Carl Hower, George DiBouno, John Simanek, and Bob Williams; and my colleagues at St. John's University who support and share my views of teaching, technology, and the arts, especially Anoinette Durso, Alan Seeger, and Julie Levinson.

Family and friends are often the last line of defense against total insanity when writing a book, and I thank them as well. Important notes of thanks to: Mary Anne, for her insights into the world of publishing; Joey, for his creative inspiration and fresh outlook on the arts; Colleen, just for being.

CONTENTS

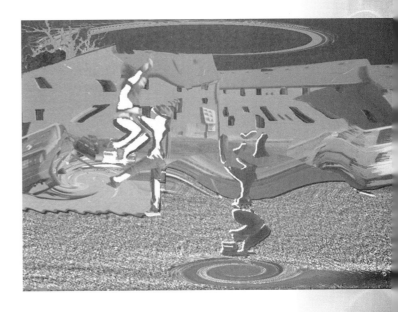

PREFACE

In April 1990, when *Computers in the Artroom* was literally hot off the press, I knew that some of the information in the book was already dated. In the four months since I had made my last changes, Apple had released its plans for the Classic and LC lines; IBM had released the 486, with talk of the 586 (now called Pentium) not far away; Voyager was working on CD-ROM titles; and there was talk from Kodak about putting images on CD. Beyond the computer industry, the television industry was working on HDTV, and AT&T was in the process of installing fiber-optic cable in various areas of the country.

It's now almost ten years later. This is, more or less, an update to *Computers in the Artroom* or what some friends have called *Son of Computers in the Artroom!* While this book builds on *Computers in the Artroom*, it expands on technologies and provides more discussion of artists and aesthetics. There are new resources, more information, more images. And, of course, there is a section on the World Wide Web.

Yet this is more than an update. The original reason for writing a book on computers was the excitement that filled my students and me when working with computers (and that was the Apple IIe!). My students and I now work in both Macintosh and Windows environments. We work with audio and video, creating multimedia presentations, and produce professional-looking publications. We use scanners, digital cameras, CD-ROM, videodiscs, VCRs, the Internet, and more, all without hesitation. And, we've changed.

The computer is not the focus of our art program; it's just another aspect of it, although an important one. We sometimes use the computer to work out ideas, and working with the computer sometimes inspires or nurtures ideas. We use the computer to experiment, to work out design considerations, typography, color, interactions of shapes and spaces, and so on. For some, the computer has become the medium of choice, and the emphasis here is on the word *choice*. We use the computer to explore images and information stored on CD-ROM: collections of museums and galleries from around the world. The computer is used to access the Web for research and to interact with people around the globe. We view art in galleries we'd never visit in person, talk with students from other parts of the country who are working on projects like our own, and, on occasion, "chat" with an artist—all without leaving the artroom.

This book tries to put technology into perspective and make it accessible for teachers, particularly art teachers, *now*. There are guidelines and discussions on incorporating the use of computers into your art curriculum, examples and activities, and lots of images. Most of this is practical. If you want to use computers and other technologies within your art program, you have to feel comfortable doing so. Some of this, however, may seem overwhelming.

In *Computers in the Artroom,* a recurring warning was: don't panic! You will see it here too. There's another warning that's become central to my thinking about technology in art education. Although it may seem an obvious thought, it can be forgotten in the technological glitz and glitter of gizmos and gadgets: teach art. As the teacher of art, your most important task is to *teach art—*

> *not* computers,
>
> *not* software,
>
> *not* Photoshop or Kid Pix or CorelDRAW.

TEACH ART: Teach theory; teach concepts; teach aesthetics and criticism; teach design; teach drawing. Design is still design; drawing is still drawing; seeing is still seeing. Computers and related technologies are just tools you can utilize while teaching art to your students.

First and foremost, *teach art.*

INTRODUCTION

The information revolution, the superhighway, interactive digital television, fiber optics, telecommunications, teleconferencing, virtual reality, multimedia, the Web—it's easy to be overwhelmed. Looking ahead is always more stressful than looking back, so think back a minute about the technologies we now take for granted that have emerged in the past twenty years or so: cable TV, VCRs, compact discs, camcorders, answering machines, cordless phones and cellular phones, even microwave ovens.

Feel better now? It is a fact that the new technologies will deeply affect all of us. The way we work, the way we live, the way we interact with others and view the world will be forever different. I maintain an optimistic outlook. Technology is exciting, offering new options, new explorations, and new visions. And it doesn't have to overwhelm.

The technologies of the future are with us today. Yes, they will get smaller-faster-cheaper-more integrated; yes, they will alter our lives. But the technologies themselves seem to be in place, even if only in a "primitive" state. What seems to be less clear is the human factor: how we will use technology and how fast we can adapt to change. When you think about all the technology we've already incorporated in our day-to-day living, we should be somewhat reassured that this may not be as bad as it seems. We take many of the devices mentioned earlier (such as the microwave oven, answering machine, and VCR) for granted.

Can we speculate then that the full integration of technology in the artroom is only a matter of time? Perhaps. It is true that our newest art teachers will embrace technology because they have been raised with it. But even our newest teachers may not have been taught with computers, and we do tend to teach the way we've been taught. The full effects of technology on education may take quite a while to achieve full impact. This is indeed new exploration, but my bottom line is this: *don't panic!*

To be sure, new media, techniques, and forms of creative expression are emerging, but there is a rather reassuring irony at work here as well. There is a continued (although some might say renewed) interest in traditional media, the hands-on, mud-up-your-elbows kind of work that is missing from the world of electronic, digital imagery. When given a choice, students often prefer working with paper and pencils, crayons and clay. Traditional media (and perhaps also traditional teachers) will not be replaced, but we may have to make some room for an additional computer or two!

Remember this: you are still the art teacher, and you will still *teach art.*

Don't panic!

Gurneet Gujral
Butterfly Collage, *Photoshop*
Randolph High School, Morristown, NJ

Allison Newman
Seattle, *Photoshop*
Randolph High School, Morristown, NJ

Note This book is intended for anyone who is involved in, interested in, or just curious about technology. It explores advances in hardware, software, and the Internet, and includes an overview of the history of computers in the creation of creative works. There are curriculum guidelines, strategies for implementation, and studio ideas from teachers who are using technology in their art program to help get you started.

There are also thoughts from artists who are using technologies for the creation of their work, and a variety of works from students. Throughout the book are special features that address current issues and concerns. Finally, there is a reference guide, in which hardware and software are described, reference material and other resources are assembled, and legal and ethical issues are raised.

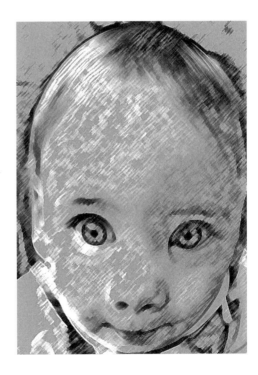

Sarah McLean
Photoshop
Randolph High School, Morristown, NJ

THE TECHNOLOGY

PART ONE

One

TECHNOLOGY: A PRIMER

Before getting into guidelines and strategies and discussing areas like multimedia and the Internet, an overview of the various technologies discussed in the book might be helpful. This is meant to be brief; more technical information can be found in Part Eight. The most important thing to remember is *don't panic!* All of this may not make sense to you right now, and you may wonder how much you need to know.

Here's the bottom line: you need a computer and a printer and some software.

It's that simple. If you are new to computers, everything else—input/output devices, video, the World Wide Web—can come later. Get some advice; talk to friends and family who have used computers; look to your students for help; and above all, don't panic!

The Computer

Clearly, of all the new technologies, the computer has had the most obvious impact. It is the driving force behind most of the technology we will look at.

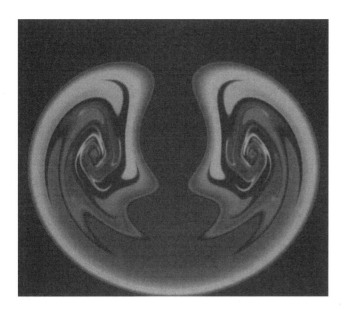

Nick Hoeing
Embryonic
Union High School, Union, MO

Alone, the computer is a powerful tool, but I think its real power is felt when it is used with other technologies, not only in creating art, but also in teaching. Computers present the artist with the possibility of expanding artistic vision, of watching ideas grow, of playing with and integrating images. In the classroom, computers have the potential of expanding the possibilities of creative expression, providing a playground for ideas and images.

Specifically, the computer package you buy today will usually include the computer itself (CPU), a keyboard, mouse, monitor, hard-disk drive, CD-RW/DVD drive, and a modem. Do you need all this? Yes.

Mac or IBM?

Because new computers are coming out so frequently, I try to avoid mentioning a particular model. When I wrote *Computers in the Artroom,* the Apple IIe was the computer most used in schools at that time, so when I had to mention a specific computer, Apple IIe it was. Now people ask, "Why did you talk about the IIe? No one has a IIe anymore." So, no matter what I say here, my comments may be doomed to obsolescence!

Here's the good news: the differences between an IBM computer and a Macintosh computer are vanishing. At this writing, when users turn on an IBM that has Windows (an operating system from Microsoft for the IBM-type computer), they are likely to comment, "Hey, it looks just like a Mac!" Further, the Macintosh can come equipped with a DOS card, which is software that allows you to run Windows programs on your Macintosh. It will be only a matter of time before the differences between machines vanish.

Bottom line? In a very few years, it really won't make much difference which machine you get. All machines will be fully compatible. To be fair, however, at the writing of this book, Macintosh computers are still the computers of preference of both artists and art teachers.

What You Need to Know

Get the fastest computers (e.g., 1 Ghz or faster) with the most memory (for example, 128–512 megabytes of RAM) and largest hard-disk drive (20–80 gigabytes) that you can afford. Yes, it's that simple! However, this does not mean that you need to get top-of-the-line machines. At this writing, the machine just described could cost less than $2,000. You must analyze your curriculum carefully: what do you intend to do with computers, and when do you intend to incorporate technology? If you are new to computers, or if you are an elementary school teacher, the top-of-the-line equipment may be more than you need. On the other hand, if you intend to incorporate video, scan images, do some desktop publishing, and so on, as many students in middle and high schools do, then you'll need more—and more powerful—machines and more of the extras.

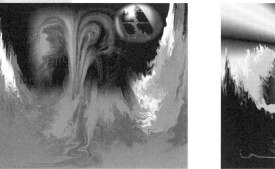

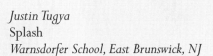

Justin Tugya
Splash
Warnsdorfer School, East Brunswick, NJ

The point is to know your needs. If you receive a budget or grant for $10,000, do you buy one computer with "the works" (laser printer, digitizer, scanner, large monitor, graphics tablet, etc.)? Or do you buy four Macs? Or six PCs?

If possible, try out the computer you intend to buy. Look at several monitors for color resolution and clarity of image, as you would a TV set. Check the feel of the keyboard. Find out about the reliability of the machine and the technical support services. (Note that reliability is very important: when a school gets a technology grant, it is often for a one-time purchase and does not cover service, repair, or upgrades.)

Where can you find some of this information? First, check the warranty of the hardware you are buying. Second, ask teachers who have been using computers what their experience has been with a particular brand or manufacturer. Third, consult computer magazines, which often include reviews of the latest hardware. The hardware is usually rated, not only in terms of performance, but also reliability.

Almost every magazine published these days also has a Web site. If you have access to the Web, go to the Web site of a magazine (www.Macworld.com, for example) and conduct a "search" of their back issues. Finally, if you are comfortable on the Web, go to ArtsEdNet or ArtsEdge and post a query on the bulletin board, or join a mailing list to get more information. (For Web addresses, see pages 136–137.)

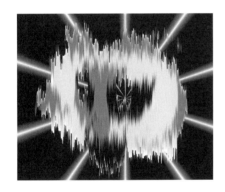  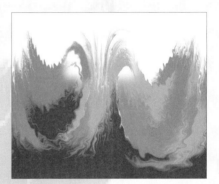

If you're looking for definitive recommendations of what to buy, sorry. This section of the book gives only an overview of what is currently available. Every school situation is different, and each piece of equipment and each software package has something to offer.

However, there is some good news: the knowledge and skills that you and your students learn when you use even the most basic graphics programs are fundamental and transferable to more sophisticated software. We teach hand-building techniques with clay before we teach the wheel; we make simple potato prints before we use a press; we weave paper before we use looms. The same is true with computers. For instance, once students have learned how to "draw" rectangles, lines, circles, and ovals on a computer, they have learned some basics that they can apply to more complicated tasks on high-end equipment.

So, does your situation call for one high-end computer, or are several computers with fewer capabilities a better choice? Do a careful analysis of the needs of your students and the constraints of your situation. (For additional information, see Part Four.)

It's very natural for us as artists and art educators to be frustrated with the many constraints of computers and computer software. Newer computers and software allow for much more flexibility, more resolution, more options—more of everything.

If you've been working with or "watching" computers over the past five years, you've already seen great advances in speed and color and control. Because we like to play as much as our students, the temptation is to buy the "best." With computers ranging in price from $800 to $3,000 and more, "the best" may not truly be the best for your students and your curriculum. Remember: Keep your students and the goals of your curriculum at the forefront of all decisions.

Garrett Visi
Clarisworks Paint
Tokeneke School, Darien, CT

Budget Considerations

Decisions concerning which computers to buy may not be left to you, the art teacher, alone. The computer coordinator may have the last word, or your school or district may have an opportunity to buy a large quantity of computers at a reduced rate. But if you can make recommendations on the final decision, the following questions may be helpful.

Consider:
- What is my current budget?
- Will I be able to purchase additional computers and software in the future, or is this my only purchase?
- Can I use equipment and software already in the school?
- What are my class sizes?
- What is the optimum number of computers?
- Where will the computers be located?
- Who will use the computers?
- Do I need a printer? A color printer? A laser printer?
- Who is responsible for repairs? Do the computers need to be insured?

Don't forget:
- Software, as well as hardware, must be purchased.
- The cost of supplies—blank disks, paper, storage boxes, ink cartridges—should be part of the budget.
- If you have to network your computers and/or printers, include the cost of cabling, switch boxes, and the like in your budget.
- The more memory a computer has, the greater the information and storage capacity. But more memory costs more money.
- A large-screen monitor is great for classroom demonstrations, but the larger the monitor, the greater the cost.
- You may need furniture for your computers.

Hardware and Software

Hardware (the actual computer and any other physical machines related to it) and software (the programs that run the hardware) are available in a myriad of choices and configurations. Part Eight gives you a comprehensive list of hardware and software, along with a brief description of the various devices and software packages.

Input

An input device is simply a piece of equipment or software that gets an image from its existing format (such as a still photo or video image) to the computer screen. Those discussed in Part Eight include the keyboard, mouse, tablet, digitizer, scanner, digital cameras, direct-to-disc photos, clip art, and photo CDs.

Output

Although there are several different ways to output images, including video and slides, the most commonly used output devices in schools are printers. Most schools use ink-jet printers and laser printers. Both are available in color and black and white. As of this writing, most art teachers are using color ink-jet printers. Plotters may also be found in schools, usually where technical drawing courses are offered.

More Than Storage, More Than Access

Zip and Jaz drives are popular forms of storage. They hold far more information than a disk and can be essential when working on large, collaborative projects with students. Some computers come with an internal Zip drive. Most computers are also equipped with a CD-RW drive. The CD-RW drive is typically used to for interactive games and learning packages, but it can also be used as a storage device.

Video can also be integrated into your computer system. DVD (Digital Versatile Disc) at the present time is being used to store full-length feature films, but can be used in a fashion similar to CD-ROM.

Software

Computers, smart as they are, are dumb! They need software (word processing, graphics, etc.) to tell them what they're supposed to be doing. Basically, you'll want to get a a variety of software packages that are on all your machines, and can be used for specific purposes. These programs range from simple

Nate Harris and Jon DeSimone
Fawn, *Streamline and CorelDrRAW*
Falmouth Middle School, Falmouth, ME

ones that rely on tools that anyone can understand and use (such as paintbrushes or scissors) to sophisticated programs that offer complex drawing tools (such as filters for special effects and compositing to rearrange image elements). Generally, more sophisticated programs emphasizing image processing, 3-D, or special effects would be used at the high school level, not only because they tend to be more expensive, but also because they require a great deal of time to learn.

However, even basic programs like Kid Pix and Painter Classic offer some of these sophisticated tools in limited form. Software typically used in art classrooms includes painting, drawing, 3-D modeling and rendering, image editing, special effects and animation, and desktop publishing. (For more about software, see page 126.)

Are you completely lost? Don't panic! If you are new to computers, all you need to know is that you need a computer, a monitor, a printer, and some software! In many schools, art teachers have little say about what will be purchased: the decisions are often school-or districtwide. But for those of you who will be making those decisions, *don't panic!*

TWO

THE IMPACT OF TECHNOLOGY ON ART EDUCATION

Technology is here, and if you haven't begun to use it in your artroom yet, get ready. It will have a profound impact on the way our students learn and the way you teach. Is that an overstatement? No. Like all teachers across the country, art teachers are feeling the effects of national and local initiatives that mandate the incorporation of technology into classroom instruction.

Some teachers have adapted gladly; others, reluctantly; some, warily. And there are still those who just plain have *not* incorporated technology at all. This is not always the fault of the teacher. For a teacher to incorporate any thing into the curriculum (whether that thing is a new textbook, medium, or technology), he or she must first understand it. That means training and time with whatever the "thing" is.

In the past, many schools bought computers, but often without any advice from experts in computers in education or from the classroom teachers. The results have been discouraging and in some cases, frustrating. For instance, some schools set up computer labs. Who used them? The math classes at first (usually for computer science); then some science classes; then a few years later, the English teachers and business teachers were using computers for writing and business applications.

In some schools where the art teacher was interested in using computers, the art classes were held in the computer lab. However, in most schools, computer labs were monopolized by a select group of teachers in a few subject areas. Some schools, after setting up a lab, put a computer in each classroom, expecting the teacher to use it. No training, no software, no budget. The computers often became dust collectors.

Until recently, computers were often found only in labs where art teachers had only limited access, limited training, and limited support. That is changing. As schools and districts recognize the need for training and support, teachers are being encouraged to pursue computer training, and some training is even being provided in the schools.

Despite this support, however, the thought of using technology can still be intimidating because we tend to teach as we've been taught, and only the most recent graduates have been taught with these new technologies. We have to learn how to use technology, and then learn how to use the technology within the art curriculum.

Caution: Danger!

It's easy to get caught up in the technology: it's glitzy; it's glamorous; and it's slick. Don't minimize that danger; it's one of my greatest nightmares. Both students and teachers can become mesmerized by what they can do with computer technologies, at the expense of good design. I have had several conversations with prospective art teachers, and when I ask them what they know, their response is a litany of software titles: "I know Photoshop and Painter and Illustrator and Quark. . ." "Wonderful," I respond, "but do you know design? Do you understand color theory? What about the elements and principles of design?"

Caution: Classroom Teachers

Many classroom teachers who have computers or computer centers in their classrooms are using graphics program like KidWorks or Kid Pix. However, they are not teaching art. The visuals students are creating on the computer are not necessarily art. Classroom teachers should not be considered art teachers because they are using this software. Art educators teach art, and classroom teachers should be encouraged to use graphics software in collaboration with the art teacher.

Most art teachers understand that teaching their students how to use the technology is not enough. They emphasize art concepts to produce good (maybe great!) student artists, not merely good technicians.

TECHNOLOGY: IT DOES BELONG
IN THE ART CURRICULUM

It is clear that more and more art teachers are using technology, but there still may be some hesitancy about why you should incorporate technology into your art curriculum. Technology may allow for new access to artists and allow the integration of other disciplines and other cultures into our classroom. What is perhaps most exciting is the integration of visual images through CD-ROMs and the Web. Technology makes possible a variety of approaches to teaching, learning, research, collaborative experiences, and problem solving. What is perhaps most exciting is the increased interaction of students with one another in the exploration of the world of art. Specifically, technology impacts

- art—the way it is created and the way we view it
- education—what students need to know, how they learn, and how we teach
- art education—what our students create, how is it created, new ways of teaching about art, and new approaches to integration with other disciplines.

New Media for Artists

Developments in technology (particularly affordable hardware and user-friendly software) have brought some artists out of the traditional studio, where they worked primarily on canvas and sketch pad, into an electronic studio, where the computer hardware and software become new tools. With technologies like computers, video cameras, scanners, and digitizers, young artists and designers can visualize their ideas and experiment with them quickly and easily.

Electronic enhancement of images from other media is possible, and new elements can be added to create composite images. Through these technologies, a new generation of art and artist is emerging. (For more about artists, see page 96.)

Furthermore, art students' access to imagery has expanded, not only through CD-ROMs, but also through the World Wide Web. On the Web, students can display their own works, look at the works of artists and other students, and even enter into collaborative projects with students from around the world.

A Critical Look

Computer-generated works are being recognized as an art form and can be seen in galleries and museums worldwide. To evaluate these new works, students need to explore the imaging potentials of computers and become critical evaluators of the resulting images. These images might best be explored from the perspective of creation and criticism.

Our students see this relatively new electronic imagery all the time. What amazed us in *Star Wars* twenty years ago, they take for granted today. The special effects in video games and in films such as *Titanic, Armageddon,* and *The X-Files* get more dazzling and spectacular with each release. Graphics are used as never before in business and industry to visualize information. Because students spend so much time looking at the imagery, they should learn to view it critically.

Playing Around: Good Ideas as the Products of Playful Thinking

Many students approach technology as artists do sketch pads—as a place where ideas can be tested and explored, a playground for ideas. Art teachers who use technology with their students have commented that the various technologies seem to restore playfulness to art. Because play is such an important part of freeing creativity, whatever encourages playing with ideas and images can be of value in art education. If students are able to play with images freely, which encourages a fuller exploration of their imaging abilities and imagination, they push and push their ideas rather than settling on the first or second version.

Trying It Again (and Again, and Again)

Playing with ideas is how greater ideas begin, but once students formulate an idea, they often approach their image with determination and precision. When working with computers, students may save their images in various stages of completion. Therefore, if a new idea is suggested by the teacher or another student, they can test it out without endangering the original image. For example, students can experiment with a number of color combinations without redrawing an image for each study. This gives the creative process a sort of risk-free dimension, allowing students to rework a sketch in a number of ways and explore alternatives before declaring a work "finished."

From Beginning to End

In large classes, some students can get lost in a back corner of the artroom for days! I sometimes find myself looking at a work and wondering where the student began and how he or she ended up with this creation. We are often forced to deal with a student's final product rather than its development or process of creating.

Again, because computers allow students to save in steps or stages, they provide both teachers and students opportunities to explore the process and decisions made in reaching that final image. Images can be discussed, analyzed, and experimented with. Criticism and suggestions may be made on the way to the final product: all the "what ifs" can be answered before students reach that final product.

Eric Messick and DJ Lyons
George Washington High School,
Danville, VA

Redefining Artistic Talent

For most students, artistic talent is defined by their ability to render objects with traditional realism. Many students have avoided art courses because they assumed that since they cannot "draw," they are not artists. Students who use technology usually come to an understanding that there is more to artistic talent than rendering objects with realism; that traditional representation is only one aspect of creativity and artistic skill. With computer technology, students often learn quickly that design is important, and layout and composition are integral to a successful image.

Or, I should say, that most students come to realize this. Some irony may be at work here. In the past few years, I've seen some students who think that just because they know how to use the computer and a graphics program (especially the more sophisticated ones, like Photoshop), they are artists. They see no need to study art or design. Some students seem to think everything that comes out of a computer is wonderful. We all have seen enough bad work to know that that is just dead wrong! Still, some do think that, and it makes the role of the art educator that much more critical.

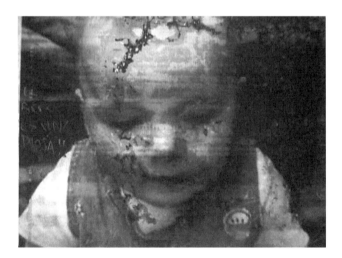

Eric Messick
Photoshop
George Washington High School,
Danville, VA

Working with Abstraction

Young children seem to have a wonderful sense of play and often appreciate abstraction, an appreciation they tend to lose as their taste becomes more sophisticated. Software like Photoshop, Painter, Painter Classic, and even Kid Pix offers students opportunities to add some "special effects" to their imagery. For example, students can "shatter" an image, or cut it up, rearrange it, and repaste it. They can "blur" a photo, add a tint, or apply an effect like mosaic or tiling.

With morphing packages, students can see how realism can distort to abstraction easily, often playfully. (One might argue that these are not created abstractions, and are more accidental than deliberate, but, as with all imagery, the key is in the discussion of the work.)

Collaboration and Integration

When you look at how fine artists and designers from all areas of the media are working these days, one thing is clear: work is a collaborative effort. For example, today a film's credits can run for five minutes, listing hundreds of names; the closing credits in a film from the 1930s or 1940s listed only five to ten names.

Very few artists who work with technology work alone. They usually need the cooperation, advice, and expertise of those inside and outside the art world to help them realize their vision. For most, this involves teamwork with visual artists, writers, engineers, technicians, and others—all working together to make a "whole" work.

Multimedia requires not only several different visual tools, but also the integration of sound and/or music and the interaction of the viewer-participant-learner. The designer has to sit down with others—the artist, the musician, the teacher—to make a good piece of software, interactive tool, game, or even a work of art. Collaboration is not a new concept for artist and art teacher—group work is often part of the curriculum—but it is becoming increasingly emphasized. Almost no one works alone anymore.

Even when working on the Web, students have the opportunity to work with other students worldwide, perhaps working to elaborate on one idea or in the incorporation of many ideas into one piece.

Katherine Allen
Falmouth Middle School, Falmouth, ME

Interdisciplinary and Multicultural Activities

The development of CD-ROM libraries and the growth of the World Wide Web (emphasis here on *world*) should encourage teachers and students to explore interdisciplinary and multicultural activities. For one thing, it's easy to do.

On the Web, students can discover artists such as Diego Rivera, Helen Cordero, or Hokusai. They can see examples of aboriginal art or the culture of Benin. Thousands of research possibilities exist.

There are a number of quality CD-ROM titles that cover art throughout the world by way of museum collections, artists, or periods. There are also titles that are not art-specific but can be used to study aesthetics and art history and criticism. Some can take students into the culture of a people or a historical period. (For CD-ROM titles, see page 134.)

Career Preparation

Multimedia technologies have found their way into business and industry, particularly the entertainment industry. Graphic artists are at work in video and film, and in desktop and electronic publishing. They work in advertising agencies, public-relations firms, and corporations. They create presentations and reports for an audience of twenty, 200, or 20 million.

Still, not all that has been created is good. Business and industry are looking for people with artistic sensibilities who have been taught how to use new technologies—and use them well. Our students, whether art majors or not, will be entering this world of desktop publication and multimedia. To be prepared for a computer-based society, they need guidance, not only in using technology, but also in design, layout, and aesthetic sensibilities.

Brittney Wyatt
Pop Art
High Mountain Road School, Franklin Lakes, NJ

GUIDELINES FOR COMBINING
TECHNOLOGY AND THE ARTROOM

For years, I have hesitated at the thought of advising teachers on how to use technology in their classroom, sure that if just shown what technology can do, they should be able to make that leap themselves. While it's true that the individual teacher is the only person qualified to make decisions concerning classroom management, it is also true that computers and related technologies are completely new to many teachers today. Help, advice, and direction are welcomed, invited, and perhaps even necessary.

First and foremost, be patient, and *don't panic!*

Now that that's taken care of, consider some guidelines.

•   **Get some experience with technology**. You don't have to be proficient in using computers. You just need to know how to turn a computer on and off, and how to use some simple software. Even the simplest programs, such as Kid Pix, contain the basic tools and operate in a manner similar to more sophisticated software. True, some equipment is very sophisticated and complicated and technical and . . . frightening! But full mastery of the computer, the video equipment, the CD-ROM, the scanner, and every software package on the market is not necessary to get started. You don't have to be an expert.

Adult education programs often offer introductory workshops on graphics programs. (See page 14,

"A Few Words on Training.") For those of you who already have some working knowledge of computer technology and want to know more, read. Go to a large bookstore or library, and browse through the various magazines, like *PC World* or *Macworld*. For something less technical, start with *Mac Home Journal*, especially if you teach younger children.

Most of these magazines include software and hardware reviews and give advice on using and troubleshooting your computer. The trade magazines are a bit more complicated, but they are well respected in their reviews and forecasts of technology. *MacWeek* and *PC Week* have up-to-date reporting on new releases of software and hardware. The Web is also a great source of information. The "For Dummies" books are novice-friendly and are written with a sense of humor. (For more specific recommendations, see page 131.)

•   **The more you know, the better; but you don't have to know everything.** Remember that you are the art teacher and not the computer teacher or the director of information services. Although you will need help in selecting hardware and software for your curriculum and artroom, try not to let others make the decisions for you. Make sure that, at the very least, you have input. And remember: you don't have to have top-of-the-line equipment and software in your classroom.

•   **Go on a fact-finding mission.** Find out what is available and what the school's future plans are. You may find that there is equipment in areas where it is not being used. It may sound odd, but it happens. There have been a number of instances in which a coordinator or principal was delighted to find a teacher interested in using the technology that another teacher had "abandoned." Although there

Hillary Scott
Clarisworks Paint
Tokeneke School, Darien, CT

Paul Straatman
Shapes Floating on the Desert
Union High School, Union, MO

certainly is no guarantee that this will happen, you never know! You might find that your district or school is involved in pursuing grant money. If so, input from you as the art teacher might be welcomed. Ask around. Talk to parents; they can be a helpful resource.

• **Your students do not have to use computers every minute of every class.** Actual use of the computer will depend on many things, including grade level, student familiarity with computers, number of available computers, and most important, the art lesson. You may go for several days or weeks with very little computer use, and then go through a period when it is never off. Use of technology should be curriculum driven. Don't panic at the thought of planning computer activities. In time, incorporating technology into your curriculum will feel more natural. Start with some simple exercises, and let the students play with the software you have.

You *may* find that the computer is used most of the time, but you have to be comfortable with this as well. For example, if you have only one computer in your room, an assignment to be done of the computer will take the entire class a considerable amount of time. You might want to use the computer as a research tool, using CD-ROMs or the Internet.

• **You, as teacher, do not have to use the computer all the time, either.** The basics of art instruction—the elements and principles of design and composition—can be taught by using computer technology, but they don't have to be. Sometimes the computer should not be used. You must feel comfortable with the tools you are using.

Some time ago, I gave a workshop in a school district for K–12 art teachers. Dabbler had just been released. Because I think it's such a wonderful tool, I suspect I was too enthusiastic in presenting the various tools to these teachers. "Look," I demonstrated, "the media most of you use and feel comfortable with are right here in the tool drawer—pen, crayon, marker." "Wait a minute," said one of the teachers. "Why would you use the computer as a pen or crayon or marker? Why not just use the pen, crayon, or marker?" I stopped. Even I can get caught up in all that computer technologies can do, but, no, they cannot replace pen, crayon, or marker—nor would I want them to.

Again, my point is that neither you nor your students have to use the computer twenty-four hours a day, every day.

• **A computer can be used as more than an art tool.** You can use it for display, research, multimedia projects, and more. With computers, you and your students can write papers, create databases of information, edit video, and create a slide show of student work. You can create a newsletter or brochure of your art program or one in conjunction with a school or community activity. You and your students can work with CD-ROMs to do research or to study the lives and works of various artists. Students can create their own disc portfolio. Use the Web to set up an alternate display area for student works or to explore works by students from around the country and around the world. "Surf" to a museum or gallery; "talk" to an artist; get information about an exhibit. Enter into a collaborative work with other Web users. The list is continually growing.

• **But always, the focus is on art.** You're the art teacher: teach art. Never lose sight of what you do. The computer should not be the focus of your curriculum. The versatility of the computer leads some teachers to the (wrong) assumption that computers will take over the artroom. They won't.

Consider an objective of your art curriculum and think about what media might be best used for a particular project. You may look around your artroom and see those two or three computers in the corner, and yet you may still decide that the pencil is the best medium to use! Think of the computer as an addition, not a replacement. More and more artists are mixing media, turning to computers and photography and printmaking and acrylics, and so on. Remember: teach art.

Ann Chen
Collected Images, *Photoshop*
Randolph High School, Morristown, NJ

A Few Words on Training

Okay, so you really believe you should be using the computer in your curriculum, but the question remains, how? We tend to teach as we've been taught, and the crux of the problem is that we weren't taught with computers.

Where can we get help?

Teachers at workshops have made one point clear: many art teachers who use computers are self-taught. They have found help from fellow teachers or their own students. With few guidelines available, they have drawn from their experiences and instinct to set realistic goals and developing lessons. However, most teachers need additional help. There are a number of places where you can get help and training.

•   Your state department of education might sponsor workshops for teachers of various levels and/or disciplines. The National Art Education Association offers several hands-on computer workshops at its national conference.

•   The computer coordinator or computer teacher at your school might be a valuable resource for solving specific technical problems.

•   Your most reliable sources will be fellow art educators who have been working with computers. They can offer you valuable guidelines and pertinent information.

•   University and college education departments offer courses in computer applications. Look for courses that deal with graphics software.

•   Your students may be a valuable resource: many of them grew up with computers and have been using them for years.

•   Companies throughout the country offer workshops on specific software packages, usually the high-end packages like Photoshop and Illustrator.

•   Look for user groups. Many states have special-interest groups of professionals and "hackers" who are willing to share their expertise with others. In some cases, they will even come into schools and offer workshops for both teachers and students. On the East Coast, there are two large user groups for the Macintosh: New York Mac Users' Group (NYMUG) and Boston Mac Users' Group (BMUG). Both organizations offer software-specific workshops.

•   Search the Web.

Be Patient

Some computer courses may overwhelm you with information unrelated to art and art education. Computer graphics courses taught in college and university art departments may use high-tech equipment that is not relevant to the computers found in schools.

Art-education departments are only beginning to address the use of computers in art education. Check course descriptions carefully before enrolling. Workshops too can be frustrating, but from many years of both taking and giving them, I have found that if I learn just one piece of information, the time has been well spent.

Start slowly, and be patient. You have to search for your own answers and rely on your best judgment. But you've done that before, with the new kiln, loom, or camera. The same principles apply here. Start slowly, maybe by using the computer in an assignment you have made before, but replacing the traditional medium with this new one.

You may want to first experiment with a small group of students, perhaps after school or with students in a gifted-and-talented program. Take your time, and be patient. Both you and your students will need some time to get used to the equipment and software. Know your students; know your program; use the new equipment so that you feel relatively comfortable with it. Everything else will follow.

Take Heart, and Don't Panic

Are computers worth this investment of time and energy? I have to yell a resounding yes! Absolutely! We have been asked to readjust our thinking and methodologies before, whether because of a cut in our department, increased class size, or a change in the philosophy of the school.

If you feel that it is important that computers be used in your curriculum, you'll find a way. Be aware of what computers can do. Can they do things that are not possible with other media? Yes. Can they help your students? Yes. Is it worthwhile to consider their use in your curriculum program? Yes. Although I attempt to address these questions throughout this book, in the end, it all comes down to this: you have to take the risk, take the time, and make an investment in the future—but what an investment!

Don't panic! You're not alone.

Annie McBride
Monsters
High Mountain Road School,
Franklin Lakes, NJ

Emma Howard
Wild West
High Mountain Road School,
Franklin Lakes, NJ

THE NEW TECHNOLOGIES

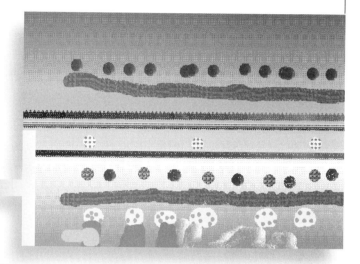

Three

You've probably seen the "For Dummies" series of books from IDG Books. Years ago, before computers, some of us might have been offended by the reference to our mental capacity; now, I'm not embarrassed to say I own a few of the books! In *Mac Multimedia & CD-ROMs for Dummies,* Deke McClelland begins his definition of multimedia by saying: "'Big Tub of Media' just doesn't have the same ring!" I almost wish it did, because multimedia can have a rather ominous ring to it. The problem may be that the term is rather vague. Exactly what is multimedia?

It's really simple; once you combine several media, you've got multimedia. Artists have been working in multimedia for years. We called it "mixed media," and it referred to combining two or more media, perhaps watercolor and pencil applied to an etching or photograph. In the audio-visual world, multimedia is the combination of sight and sound, usually controlled by a computer.

Stephanie K. Snyder
Photoshop
Randolph High School, Morristown, NJ

Kelly Turso
Photoshop
Randolph High School, Morristown, NJ

Multimedia generally means that software includes some or all of the following:
- full-motion video
- still images
- animation
- graphics
- text
- audio

It really is that simple.

The combinations range from simple to complex, and the product may be one-way communication or an interactive program. Because the definition is rather broad, just combining one or more of these media allows some software publishers to say that their package is multimedia when, in fact, it merely combines text and graphics. This can be deceiving. "True" multimedia is something more.

Things You Should Know

When I was writing this chapter, I found that I was grouping things into two areas: *using* multimedia (CD-ROMs) for history and research and aesthetics, and *creating* multimedia works and presentations.

Using multimedia refers to using programs and CD-ROMs and even the Web to enhance the learning experience, especially (but not only) when this includes history, research, and aesthetics. The section on using multimedia includes what you need in order to take advantage of the various programs available, gives you a guide to assessing the quality of those programs, and offers some ideas on how you might incorporate the various packages into your art program.

Creating multimedia includes combining any of the technologies and media to create a work, especially when that includes utilizing various software packages to create or display artworks. Creating multimedia can also be a simple combination of any kind of information into a well-organized multimedia presentation. The section on creating multimedia includes a discussion of equipment used in creating multimedia works, and suggests some guidelines on the design and completion of a multimedia work.

Susan Goss
George Washington High School,
Danville, VA

Don't Panic!

There are several things you should know about multimedia right from the start.

- It's not as complicated as it sounds. Multimedia simply means "many media," and it's not all that different from mixed media. Anytime you combine images with sound and/or text, you have multimedia.
- Multimedia doesn't have to be costly to use or create.
- Multimedia can offer you and your students a wonderful outlet for bringing talents and talented people together.
- Creating multimedia works can be can be easy or difficult, depending on what you're trying to do. Further, you don't have to create multimedia works, but it's worth learning how.
- Your students will likely find it much easier to work with and create than you will.
- There are great CD-ROMs and Web sites available for you and your students to use both as research tools and as models for your works. Have I lost you yet? Stay with me, and *don't panic!*

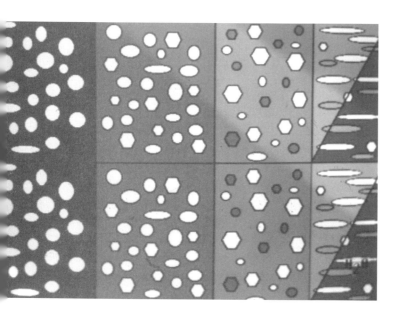

Will Winston
Trip to the Center of the Earth
University of Northern Colorado
Greeley, CO

USING MULTIMEDIA

Multimedia and Learning About Art

As teachers, we know there are many different learning styles. If advances in technologies, developments in interactive multimedia, and research into areas like artificial intelligence and virtual reality have done anything to change education, perhaps it is the change in attitude towards learners.

When technologies are used well, they offer students the option of finding their own path through exploration and discovery. This is true not just in art education, but also in all other disciplines. Clearly, the computer can be used with other media in the creation of artworks, the development of interactive lessons, and so on, but, at the very least, art teachers can make use of the computer and arts-related CD-ROMs to encourage students to use the computer to explore history, research, and aesthetics.

Multimedia is powerful and exciting. The ability to store vast warehouses of information in a variety of forms is only the beginning. This information does not have to be literal and linear, but can be visual and "mosaic." The book, no longer the exclusive source of information and knowledge, is joined by film, video, animation, and sound. Learners can browse and research, and arrange and coordinate information. Moreover, they can take responsibility for their own learning.

Educators—and perhaps art educators especially—have known for years that multimedia offers more ways to relate content to a student's personal experiences: there is more variety of content in terms of audio, video, and so on; and greater flexibility in using content to suit learning styles and individual needs. Multimedia can bring content to life. It can personalize material and make it relevant. It can create linkages where none existed or, conversely, isolate things for clarity.

Movies, video, sound, and animation become part of the learning process. Teacher and student can move from passive to active learners to become actors, not just reactors. Students themselves can develop lessons, write papers that access a variety of sources, and add their own unique spin to the exploration and the learning.

Imagine having immediate access to images of art from all over the world. There are high quality CD-ROMs and videodiscs featuring works from the Metropolitan Museum of Art, the National Gallery, and the Louvre. Your students can see not only an artist's paintings, but also what inspired him or her. They can hear some of the artist's own thoughts, see the world he or she lived in, and even watch the artist at work.

What a teacher can do with such expanded access to imagery and information is multifold. A new world of study is possible. Imagine being able to enter Picasso's studio while he's working on a masterpiece, perhaps stopping to have a conversation with him while he works. Impossible? Well, a real-time conversation isn't possible, but letters, writings, interviews, and film footage of the artist at work enable the user to have a sense of actually being in the artist's world and a "virtual" interview might be possible.

Hope Dector
Steve I, *Photoshop*
Randolph High School, Morristown, NJ

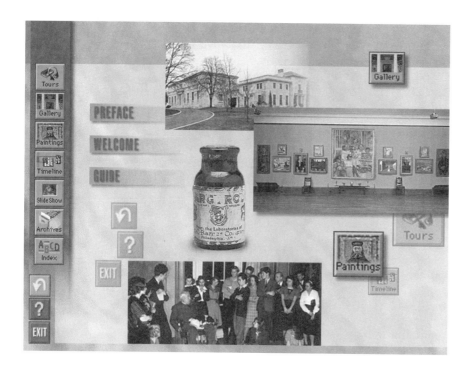

A Passion for Art provides the viewer with a tour of the Barnes Foundation, one of the greatest private collections of Post Impressionist art. This opening screen from the CD shows the viewer some of the many options available, including background information on the Foundation (preface), a welcoming message, and a guide for using the CD. Courtesy of Forest Technologies.

CD-ROMs

A few years ago, you brought your stereo system toward state-of-the-art sound by buying CDs and a CD player: digital sound with music perfectly reproduced. Now, it seems as though everyone has a CD *changer*, which costs about the same as your single player! A CD drive is now standard on most computers, and the titles available for use at work, home, and school grow each day.

A Brief Overview
In 1982, just a few years after videodiscs made their debut, compact discs (CDs) were introduced as an audio-delivery medium. This format—unlike the videodisc, which stores an analog signal—stores digital information. For the first few years, the CD-ROM industry took advantage of the large volumes of information that could be put on a disc—the equivalent of 250,000 typed pages!

CD-ROMs are easier to store and cheaper to produce than all that paper. Consequently, *Grolier's Encyclopedia* became a logical choice for a CD-ROM. All that information, all those volumes could be condensed to one disc. Furthermore, the discs could be updated regularly and cheaply. Libraries and archives started putting their catalogs and indices on disc.

In the early 1990s, CD-ROMs changed dramatically from a text-based database to full-color multimedia with high quality sound and graphics. Their first intrusion was in the form of games, but more was to come.

CDs: More Than Music
A compact disc is the disc itself. A CD holds incredible amounts of information: over 600 MB of information, or almost as much information as 600 diskettes. We've all heard audio CDs and know that they store up to seventy-five minutes of music, but CDs can hold any digital information. And that's where CD-ROM comes in. CD-ROMs are read-only memory, which means that you cannot write, alter, or save information on them. Although writable drives are becoming more affordable, it will be a while before they are commonplace (for more information, see page 125).

A CD-ROM is used to augment, not replace, the hard drive. The advantage of these discs is that they are removable, have a large storage capacity, and are more durable than diskettes.

Because of the storage capacity of CD-ROMs, they have become a preferred media for the distribution of a variety of information including books—especially multivolumes like Grolier's Encyclopedia—databases of information such as those you find in libraries, and software. CD-ROMs eliminate the need for dozens of diskettes, photography, and video or film clips.

The large storage capacity and versatility of CD-ROMS means that multimedia programs on CD can combine information in a variety of ways, allowing for user interaction. Encyclopedias can contain speeches and video clips. Software can include demonstrations on the use of software.

Into the Artroom

CD-ROMs, then, can be an exciting resource in the artroom. Some art-specific titles are *With Open Eyes; A Passion for Art: Renoir, Cézanne, Matisse and Dr. Barnes; The Louvre Museum; Vincent van Gogh: Life and Works; Leonardo da Vinci; Painters Painting;* and *Comic Book Confidential.* These are only some of the titles, and more programs are in development. Most cost between $30 to $50, and many of these disks run on both Mac and Windows.

For more resources, look to other disciplines, like geography, history, science, and language arts for titles you might find of interest in your art curriculum. Most of the encyclopedias include not just textual information on art and artists but images as well.

CD-ROMs created for social studies feature images from periods in history, like the Industrial Revolution, Word War II, or the civil rights movement in America.

Along with maps, geography CD-ROMs contain wonderful images of countries and regions. Science offers another resource where students can explore images from space, our own world, and the human body. And there are language arts programs that explore topics ranging from Greek mythology to contemporary American literature. While these CDs may not be art specific, they can offer students an opportunity to explore the influences of a period of time or an area of the world on art images and art making.

Even the young-reader series like *Reader Rabbit, JumpStart,* or the *Disney Animated Storybook Collection* can be fun for students to explore, not only in their own right but in terms of making some observations and criticisms about the quality and appropriateness of the images used. Many titles created specifically for children contain wonderfully engaging animation, music, riddles, and games that could be used as models for children who want to create their own multimedia presentations. For example, the Living Book series from Broderbund features children's books that

The Louvre Museum is an interactive CD-ROM designed for the elementary school child. Simple icons and interface allow children easy access to some of the wonderful art works housed at the Louvre. Courtesy of Forest Technologies.

encourage children to explore. When they click on a door, it opens; select a character and it will sing or talk; birds fly and dogs bark. These titles are cleverly done and are filled with ideas that students, young and old, can build on.

Evaluating CD-ROM Titles: The Good, the Bad, and the Waste of Time and Money

You would think that CD-ROMs would naturally be well designed, but some definitely are not. Designing for screen is different from designing for print, and, even visually, some titles are just plain awful. Further, designing for interactive learning and taking advantage of all that CD-ROM and computer technology can do is a relatively new area. But just because it can be done, doesn't mean it will be done well.

Although CD-ROMs are not expensive, there's no point in throwing away money. How do you know if a particular CD-ROM is worth buying for your curriculum? The good news is that there are a lot of titles to choose from. There are a number of things to look for in a CD-ROM.

- **Ease of Use:** Can you simply install the CD and use it immediately? Are directions needed? If they are, are they easy to follow? Is it clear how to control sound? What is the quality of the images? Although most publishers take great care in the reproduction of images, some are not as clear as they should be, or the color in some is slightly off.

- **Clarity of Text:** Is the accompanying text easy to read? Look for a glossary and index. Is the included reference material appropriate to the grade level? Of course, if you are getting a disc for yourself, and not for classroom use, grade-appropriate text is not relevant, but you should make sure that the text is clear and easy to follow.

- **Quality of Sound:** Many CD-ROMs include sound—in the form of music; the audio version of text; or the pronunciation of names, places, and titles. If the sound is not clear or if you cannot adjust it, this can be a problem, particularly if you intend to use the disc with students. Check to see if there is an option to turn the sound off. If several students are looking at CD-ROMs while you're teaching, you may find yourself competing with several narrators!

- **Screen Design:** Is the design of the screen inviting? Is there a center of interest, or is there so much going on that the viewer may have trouble finding information? Has color been selected so that text is easy to read and images are shown to their advantage? Can you find what you are looking for on the screen? Can you go back and forth from screen to screen or to your "home" page easily?

- **Quality of Instruction and Information:** Overall, is the CD inviting? How easily are you able to move through the program? Can you find things you were looking for? Is there a "tour" or a model available so that you could be guided through the disc? Are you able to control the sequencing of what you are viewing? Are you able to easily access the images and information you want? Are you able to download information? Is there a help button? Do you have to see the credits every time you use the disc? Can you exit the program easily?

Do you have to preview every CD-ROM title? Well, you should, but that assumes there are thirty-five hours in a day. *SchoolArts* and *Arts and Activities* sometimes have reviews of art-related titles. A few CD-ROM publishers, including Forest Technologies and The Getty Foundation, have had booths at the National Art Education Association (NAEA) conference and display a variety of discs. For additional resources, look to the Web and other art teachers. (For Web sites, see page 132).

When I teach workshops, I often bring a handful of CD-ROMs and invite art teachers to look at them. However, finding reviews or previewing the discs before you buy them is not as easy as going to a bookstore or library. You might want to ask your state association to sponsor a workshop just to look at or "swap" CD-ROMs.

CD-ROMs in the Art Curriculum

The various CD-ROMs available can be used in two ways: by you, the teacher, for discussion, in much the same way that you would use slides or prints; or by students for their own investigation and research.

For Teachers: CDs are an excellent addition to your slide collection! Of course, if you don't have a means of projecting the image or have access to a large-screen monitor, using a CD-ROM as you would use slides is a bit impractical. On a 15" monitor, the image is just too small for viewing by a class. But if you do have a means of making the image large enough so that all students can see it, you can make use of the variety and quality of images available on CD-ROMs.

You can explore the collected works of a gallery or museum, or focus on a particular artist, style, or period. Sometimes, this is easy: just choose a disc on Cézanne or van Gogh or Leonardo. At other times, you may want to use the images on a disc to create your own presentation, but not necessarily in the given sequence. For example, you might want students to explore a particular element of art, like line or color, by looking at the way artists have emphasized those elements in their works. You could access *With Open Eyes,* a wonderful disc for elementary-school students that allows you to actually create your own "album" of images from the disk in your own database. So, as you look through the disc, you might select a work by Orozco, Picasso, and Cézanne to illustrate use of the art element.

Or, you might divide students into small groups and have them look at *With Open Eyes* and create their own album of images to show the class at a later time. Not all discs are quite so friendly, but you certainly can access the images in a sequence that you determine, not unlike pulling slides of prints for a class lesson or presentation.

For Students: Students can use the vast storehouse of images and information on CD-ROMs as a resource tool or a means of exploration. A well-designed disc does not limit the users to linear access. In other words, students can start up a CD-ROM and explore the artist or gallery, for instance, in a way that interests them—they are in control.

With Open Eyes: Images from the Art Institute of Chicago is one of the top-selling art-related CD-ROM titles. With over 200 works of art from the Art Institute of Chicago, this inviting CD-ROM takes the viewer into the world of art in an inviting, nonthreatening way.

The main menu or screen starts off with a different picture each time you start the disk. This can work well with young children since it starts them off in a different spot every time they use the disk. Further, if they are looking for a particular picture, it's easy to find.

- An information bar located at the top of the screen brings you to textual information on the artist and the artwork.

With Open Eyes. *Courtesy of Forest Technologies*

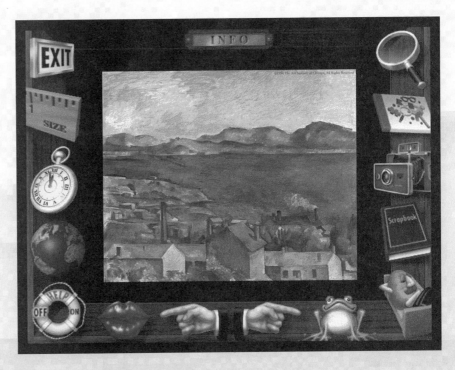

This screen, from A Passion for Art, *is a partial view of one gallery. The diagram below the gallery wall shows the viewer where he or she is in relation to the gallery. The viewer may turn and look at another wall of this gallery or select a painting on the wall. Once selected, the painting is enlarged and appears with information about the painting and artist. Note the option bar on the left side. The viewer can click an icon for additional information, help, or to jump to another section of the CD. Courtesy of Forest Technologies.*

- A ruler takes you into a virtual gallery to get a sense of the size and scale of the work.
- A stopwatch takes you to a timeline.
- The globe takes you to a map, which in turn takes you to the images available from various countries.
- A scrapbook brings you to a section where you can create your own portfolio or scrapbook of images (and later play them back.)
- The magnifying glass enlarges the image to full screen.

This well-designed CD-ROM was created with elementary children in mind and although it can be used with older students, the icons are meant to be playful and could tire a teenager. Still, *With Open Eyes* is a wonderful, fun tool for art teachers to use to introduce students to the world of art. Teachers can use it with their class or allow students to use it on their own—it's that easy to use.

A Passion for Art is a wonderful tour of what is considered by some the greatest private collection of Post-Impressionist paintings in the world. Well-designed and image-rich, this is a more complex CD than *With Open Eyes*. I would suggest it for middle and high school students.

The homepage of *A Passion for Art* includes a welcome and a guide to the Barnes Foundation. Students can take a look at the homepage or go directly to one of the other seven sections:

- Tours: There are four tours, including "Dr. Barnes and the Foundation"; "Gallery Tour"; "The Female Nude"; and "*The Dance* by Matisse." The tours can run up to fifteen minutes in length, but you can access them in smaller segments, so if students do not have time to finish a tour, they can return to the section where they left off and not have to start from the beginning.
- Gallery: The Gallery places the viewer in the virtual gallery, which replicates the actual Barnes Foundation; you can see paintings "hung" in the gallery, allowing for comparisons with other paintings in terms of placement and size. You can also select one of the paintings and get information on the painting and the artist.
- Paintings: Access information about individual works including close-ups, a portfolio of all works by an artist in the Barnes Collection, and a biography of the artist.
- Timeline: Pictures on a timeline with corresponding historical events. There is a great deal of information here and it can get a bit confusing.
- Slide Show: Students can select an image and create their own slide show of works.
- Archives: View documents in the collection including correspondence and financial receipts

about the paintings, blueprints of the Foundation, and more.

- Index: Access to information or work by artist or title.

All in all, this is a well-designed CD that allows the viewer to either be led through the various sections of the Foundation or to select particular images and determine the pace and scope of a "visit."

If a CD-ROM is well designed (and that is the key), it is designed for *random* access and allows users—students and teachers—to control the exploration of information. Can you do that with a book? Yes, but it's not nearly as much fun; and the CD-ROM animation, video clips, and quality of sound and image can't be matched by books.

WHATEVER HAPPENED TO VIDEODISC?

Videodiscs (laserdiscs) are still around, and film aficionados have them!

Videodisc is to images what an audio compact disc (CD) is to music . . . and more. Most videodiscs are about the size (12 inches) of a 33 1/3 record album, but have the characteristic sheen of compact discs. To play a CD, a CD player uses a laser, a beam of light that reads the information off the disc. Nothing touches the disc itself, so there is no erosion of the CD. To play a videodisc, a videodisc player (which can be attached to your TV or monitor) reads the information in a similar manner, so the integrity of the visual image is maintained. Videodiscs used for education and training store up to 54,000 still frames (images or text) or thirty minutes of motion video per side. Those frames can be accessed in any order, almost instantly. Further, videodiscs have a soundtrack so you can listen to commentary about the collection of images you are viewing, whether a historical survey, stories about the artists, or aesthetic discussions.

The difference between a videodisc and a CD is in the way that each stores information. The videodisc plays analog signals, so you can play full-motion video, such as

a movie. A CD-ROM, because it stores information digitally, must compress video information. While the CD-ROM is exceptional for sound and text—even still images and animation—the video compression is not yet what it will become, and full-motion video is difficult to store on CD-ROM. Usually, a CD-ROM contains no more than ten minutes of full-motion video while a videodisc can hold up to two hours of full motion video. Because a CD-ROM drive is part of most any computer system you buy, it has become the preferred method of delivery . . . for now. DVD is gaining ground. Yes, another new technology; its programming and design are similar to current CD-ROM technology.

The future of videodiscs is not bright. There are few, if any, new titles in development, and manufacturers have discontinued the development of the videodisc player. If you already have a videodisc player, don't panic. The distributors I spoke with said they would continue to carry titles until there were no more in stock. Further, if you already have a few titles, the videodisc itself is virtually indestructible, and you should be able to use it with your classes for years.

So, *don't panic!*

CREATING MULTIMEDIA

Do I have to "teach" multimedia?

No! But our students are *using* this multimedia stuff, and they will *create* it as well. The question is not if we should teach multimedia to our students but who should teach them. If art educators fail to meet the challenge, someone else will meet it: the computer coordinator, media specialist, or maybe the faculty member who just isn't afraid to tackle something new.

However, we should address what is being created. There are some not-so-great works coming from schools—and not just from students, but from teachers too. And who is the visual expert if not you? Not all that is prepared commercially is of the highest caliber either, so you might first teach students just to look at software and evaluate it critically.

I think the teaching of multimedia falls in the domain of art education, not only as an art form in its own right, but also as a new way of presenting information. And yes, this might be a long and tedious process; but it is also a collaborative, integrating process that incorporates a multitude of talents and people if the work is to be good. You need writers and planners and designers and camera people and graphic artists and sound engineers and a director, and . . . well, you get the idea.

But do *you* have to do it? No! But you should really think about it. You don't have to create the quintessential interactive program. A simple presentation that combines sound and images is fine. And you don't have to be a technical expert: you could create a slide show with sound on Kid Pix! (By the way, you can also incorporate animation and video in Kid Pix.)

Dana Mistretta
Photoshop
Randolph High School, Morristown, NJ

Victoria Batha
Clarisworks Paint
Tokeneke School, Darien, CT

Are you going to explain everything I need to know here?

No, but I will go over some of the basics, and I will tell you where to go to get some great information. My best advice is to go to a bookstore and look for information on creating multimedia. One of my favorites is the "For Dummies" series from IDG Books. These books are fun and a bit irreverent, and they assume you know next to nothing. You can skip around and find just what it is you need to know, or start at the beginning and go straight through. Try *Mac Multimedia and CD-ROMs for Dummies,* by Deke McClelland.

You might want to look at some titles from Peach Pit Press, such as *Designing Multimedia,* by Lisa Lopuck. If you want help with a specific piece of software, there are several books for that. For example, if you use HyperStudio, try *Help I Have HyperStudio . . . Now What Do I Do?* Another good series is *Technology for Terrified Teachers* from Teacher Created Tools, which includes *HyperStudio for Terrified Teachers, Kid Pix for Terrified Teachers,* and *ClarisWorks for Terrified Teachers.* (For more resources, see Part Eight, page 131.)

More Than Games

When my students think of CD-ROMs, their thoughts go immediately to games. Although this book is about education, let's be honest: when our students are not in school and are busy working on the computer, chances are they're either on the Web or playing some sort of game. Our students are comfortable with the idea of combining media to create a single impression or idea or concept. Movie videos (on MTV) probably began the trend for Generation X, but arcade games, Nintendo, and Sega had their part as well.

But multimedia is more than games, and students should know that too. If used well, multimedia can give them a powerful, self-expressive tool for display or presentation of information and ideas. What is essential for students to the creation of quality multimedia programs or presentations is that they have a goal in mind and that their projects are well designed.

Ben Lafond
Arts High School, Minnesota Center for
Arts Education, Golden Valley, MN

Evan Giordanella
Franklin Avenue Middle School,
Franklin Lakes, NJ

More Equipment

For those of you who are not familiar with the hardware and software, here may be just the place to start. Even though there are lots of products, you won't feel overpowered by technical information. For those who are looking for specific technical information, Part Eight (page 120) will refer you to a number of sources. There are also resources such as educational-journal articles that focus on multimedia.

Hardware

The more you get involved in working with multimedia, the more equipment you will need, and that equipment should be upgraded if it is not new. (This equipment is explained more fully on page 121.)

Some stores like to label computers as "multimedia computers." The truth is, most computers sold today are multimedia computers—or could be with minor additions. Depending on the software you use, you need a computer with at least 256 MG of memory (more if you use a program like Photoshop) and a hard drive of at least 80 GB of memory. Most computers now come with a sound board and video capabilities. What would be nice to have is a minimum of 80 GB hard drive, 572 MG of memory, and a 17" monitor. Oh, yes, and a 1 Ghz CPU.

Although you can actually get started with much less, there is more hardware that would be *nice* to have. This includes

- scanner (preferably a flatbed scanner)
- camera (a digital still camera or camcorder)
- VCR and TV monitor (for creating video)
- microphone/sound input
- storage (a Zip drive or any other external drive that has a large storage capacity). Diskettes, which hold only 1.4 MG, are not sufficient for multimedia. There are other drives as well, including Jaz, SparQ, and Clik.
- projection system (an LCD panel; for better color, a projector or large-screen monitor)
- modem and Internet connection

Michelle Hoffman
Photoshop
Randolph High School, Morristown, NJ

Software

The software I've included is by way of suggestion, not strict recommendation. Software is upgraded frequently, and as companies merge, some is renamed or even discontinued.

- graphics software: Photoshop, Illustrator, and even Kid Pix or Kid Pix Studio
- presentation software: PowerPoint, and even Kid Pix or Kid Pix Studio
- QuickTime or Real Player (for playing movies, video, and animation in multimedia presentations)
- authoring software: HyperStudio (probably most used in schools, particularly for those who have never worked with multimedia programs) and Director (especially for high-school students and for your own multimedia development)
- editing software: Premier or Final Cut Pro
- Web browser: Netscape or Explorer
- Web software: Dream Weaver and Flash

Putting It Together

Authoring Programs

An authoring program combines text and image and sound. The release of HyperCard, an authoring language from Apple, and the later release of HyperStudio, from Roger Wagner, were real breakthroughs for many educators. Before their release, authoring software was cumbersome and difficult to use. The easy interface of HyperCard and HyperStudio with the Macintosh gave software developers, educators, and students a new tool for creating their own custom-designed multimedia packages. (HyperStudio is available for both Mac and Windows.)

Other authoring packages, such as Macromedia's Director, are also available for use with various computers, as are newer versions of HyperCard and HyperStudio. You don't have to learn an entirely new software package to get started with multimedia: you can work with some very basic packages. For example, if you teach elementary school, you might want to encourage your students to do group projects with Kid Pix.

Jacalyn Neely
Trip to the Center of the Earth
University of Northern Colorado
Greeley, CO

30

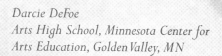

Darcie DeFoe
Arts High School, Minnesota Center for
Arts Education, Golden Valley, MN

VIDEO: COMING TO A CLASSROOM NEAR YOU

Part of the excitement for multimedia is the potential unleashed by QuickTime and Real Player although QuickTime is becoming the standard for all machines. QuickTime provides a framework for full-motion video synchronized with sound. The programs allow you to capture video and then use it, almost as you would use still images or words. They become files that can be edited, recomposed, cut, and pasted.

What this means is that a video "window" can be embedded into a lesson or student report with a sound clip or within a graphics image. Video clips can be downloaded from a CD-ROM or the Web. Lessons and assignments come alive. This easy access to video offers an opportunity to do things never done before. Students can shoot footage with a camcorder, transfer it to the computer, edit, add special effects, add audio—all at a reasonable cost.

More good news! With QuickTime VR, you can view images a full 360 degrees. Your students, using a series of still images, can loop their photos together to create their own panoramic views or to show their 3-D in-the-round works in a presentation.

Now, if you only had the time.

ANALOG? DIGITAL?

Most of today's TVs, VCRs, radios, and telephones are analog devices, which means that information is stored in a continuous stream. But digital information is stored as numbers, and it's the way things are going. The computer stores information digitally. Digital information is compressed easily and maintains its integrity. HDTV is coming to a TV near you!

Elizabeth Knight Gulliver
Splashing on Beaches in Maine, Dabbler
Falmouth Middle School, Falmouth, ME

Presentations

For two good reasons, start with a presentation package, or use the slide-show module within ClarisWorks or Kid Pix. First, you probably have the software needed. Second, a simple presentation is easy to do. If you and your students can create a presentation by organizing simple images into a logical or progressive sequence, you have a basic understanding of the beginning elements of the more complex programs.

The activity on pages 93–95 takes you and your students through the creation of a slide show in Kid Pix. The same procedures followed in Kid Pix also work in ClarisWorks and PowerPoint. Begin by having students group their works together (a storyboard of sorts) in a presentation to create a slide show. Once that's done, they might include a title slide or a screen with information about how the works were created or about each artist's intent in creating his or her work. Students might include a variety of transitions to get the viewer from one slide to the next. With pictures set and text added, some adventurous soul might like to add sound or even a QuickTime movie. Once one student does it, the rest of the class will want to do it!

Hypertext, HyperCard, HyperStudio, and HTML

"Hyper" refers to the ability to "jump" from one place to another with a click of the mouse. In the World Wide Web, these jumps are called links, which are usually words or phrases that allow you to go from page to page, linking you to other sites on the Web, or to other areas of information. (See more on Web sites on pages 47–48.)

Let's look at a program on Impressionism that you might put together for your students. HyperStudio's basic unit is a card (roughly equivalent to a screen). You download or scan in several paintings. Using HyperStudio, you create a brief biographical sketch of Monet that takes up three cards of information. You type in the text, but you can highlight words (such as the titles of the paintings you've included) within the text, thereby creating a link to another card in your presentation. This creates a button that jumps the viewer, for instance, to the painting when he or she clicks on its highlighted title.

Christopher Sullivan
Clarisworks Paint
Tokeneke School, Darien, CT

As a student reads about Monet, he or she might read straight through the information, going from page to page (card to card) in sequence until reaching the end, where you have included several of Monet's paintings. However, another student might be curious about the Water Lilies series while reading about it. The student can click on the title and jump immediately to that image.

Although I oversimplified the description, those are the basics. You can insert almost anything—text, photographs, clip art, movie clips, sound—into HyperStudio. You can even use images, sound, and movie clips from CD-ROMs or the Web.

Anna Aaker
Arts High School, Minnesota
Center for Arts Education,
Golden Valley, MN

Getting Started

First, you have to decide what it is you want to do.
- Will students work on a presentation of some kind?
- What will the presentation be of?
- Will students work individually or in groups?
- Do I want students to use all original works or to scan in images from other resources?
- Will there be text? How much?
- Sound?
- Video?
- How much time will students have for the project?

Then you have to answer some technical questions.
- What kind of access do I have to computers and other equipment (scanners, digitizing cameras, the Internet, CD-ROMs, and so on)?
- How much storage capability do I have?
- How will this be viewed (on a small screen, large monitor, or by projector)?

Once you have dealt with the technical issues, you can move to the actual creating of the project.

Start with a storyboard. A storyboard will help students plan out the text and images, as well as any sound bites they want to include in their project. Students may need to actually write a script. If the project is well planned *off* the computer, then computer time will be minimized. However, if students just jump right onto the computer and put things together in an unorganized fashion, they will spend a great deal more time on the computer trying to edit and rearrange their project. Storyboarding or pre-planning is very important and, in the end, will save everyone time. It also is very important when you only have one or two computers available.

A simple presentation made with Kid Pix or ClarisWorks can be done in an hour *if* you have all the images ready for placement. A project that incorporates sound, text, and movie clips will take longer. Most teachers have students work in groups on this kind of a project throughout the semester or year. But be forewarned: more and more students have the hardware and software to complete multimedia presentations at home and are creating some very interesting reports and presentations. Don't underestimate the talents of your students!

Is Multimedia Really Worth It?

You have to ask yourself if you want to make the considerable time investment to multimedia and if it should be part of your curriculum. There is never enough time in the school year to accomplish everything we want, and what you don't need is another project.

But multimedia is important. In my ideal world, students go to middle school with their portfolio on disc. The Kid Pix Slide Show described on pages 93–95 is not the most sophisticated your students could do. However, by completing such projects students learn to present their works (those created on computer and those 2-D images scanned into the computer) in a unified, logical way. Further, if they have written a script, they have analyzed their work, talked about it, and discussed it—and that's a valuable lesson as well.

The point? You and your students can create a multimedia presentation with limited resources. You can use a simple program like Kid Pix to create any number of projects. Of course, Kid Pix is limited, and there are other software programs you could use. Many of them you may already have access to.

ClarisWorks allows you to create a slide show. HyperCard gives you an opportunity to create "stacks," or index cards of information. It also offers hypertext, the ability to create "buttons" that allow you to link to other cards of information. HyperStudio is the preferred software package right now in elementary and middle schools because of its ability to combine text, graphics, and video; and the additional opportunity to create links to other "pages." Many teachers use HyperStudio for their own projects, but those who have a large or complex project in mind will soon outgrow HyperStudio and go on to Macromedia's Director. (Caution: Director is not as simple to use as Kid Pix.)

With any of these programs, users can create portfolios of their works, visual term papers, and reports on just about any topic (an exploration of an artist, a period in art history, a particular theme or style). Furthermore, the collaboration between art teacher and classroom or subject-area teachers has produced some wonderful projects, thereby creating an interdisciplinary approach to a topic or theme. Projects have ranged from science (endangered species, weather, molecular structures) to history (timelines, the Civil War, the civil rights movement) to mathematics (3-D modeling, fractals) and even to class yearbooks on disc. The possibilities are vast.

So, is it worth it? That depends on the goals and expectations you have of your students and your curriculum.

USING VIDEO IN YOUR ARTROOM

Video production is the topic for another book, but mention of the potential that video offers your curriculum is important. Video equipment is still quite expensive. To outfit a TV studio, you need not only cameras, but also sound equipment, lights, and editing equipment—and that's just for starters.

Yet, more and more schools and school districts are investing in some or all of this equipment. In some cases, local cable TV providers either give a school equipment or allow students to use the cable company's equipment and/or facilities. Some schools have taken advantage of Channel One. This is a service provided to high schools and some middle schools, that installs a TV in every classroom—on the condition that their sponsored fifteen-minute news program be watched by all students every day. There are several reasons that not all schools agree to carry Channel One. One reason is that the service includes two to three minutes of advertising in its programs.

With a TV in almost every classroom, many schools have a small TV studio where students produce a school news report, which, at the very least, broadcasts the traditional announcements heard in homerooms or first-period classes. If TV equipment is in place, you may have the opportunity to use video in your art program. Camcorders have become more affordable, and you may have a noble parent who will let a son or daughter bring a camcorder to school. Students can import video clips into a multimedia presentation, and can also use a program like Painter to produce some special video effects. Animation is still another possibility.

Tackling video production is a major challenge for any teacher. However, consider the possibilities, particularly at the high-school level. We're not talking about a one-hour weekly drama here! But a project in video (or film!) provides students with a truly collaborative working experience that touches on a variety of artistic talents.

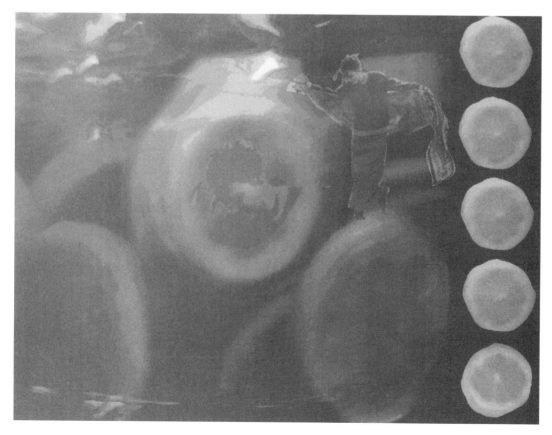

Kristin DeArruda
Arts High School,
Minnesota Center for
Arts Education, Golden
Valley, MN

Multimedia into the Twenty-first Century

To describe multimedia in the past three years, I'd use two words: growing and maturing. Several years ago, multimedia broke out of school and industry and entered the home market. Its real emphasis is on activity and interactivity—engaging the passive observer to become an active participant. In terms of the home market, that initially meant games. That market has grown, however, and recent trends show a growing demand for "how-to" and self-help titles and references. The home market has also grown to include areas to supplement school subjects. Many publishers are now targeting parents with reading, math, geography, science, history, and even some art titles. But not just parents will buy multimedia technology. Education and training will account for a large part, with education likely to carry 50 percent of the market.

Among other trends that we will probably see are
- thousands more CD and DVD titles
- dozens more improved graphics tools
- more affordable video tools, especially QuickTime, QuickTime VR, and the new DVD (which holds two hours of full motion, more information than a CD-ROM)
- more storage capacity
- faster equipment and less cost
- better, faster, and more World Wide Web access and increased interactivity on the Web
- digital television for more access, better image quality, improved compression, and improved QuickTime capabilities
- More web sites! Nearly every museum has a web site and they are loaded with art images, and most are well designed.

Brian Miner
Photoshop
Union High School, Union, MO

Using and Creating Multimedia

For art educators, one of the most important aspects of multimedia is what the availability of images on CD-ROMs and DVD affords us. At the very least, students can have access to clear images of thousands of pictures, sculptures, buildings, artifacts, jewelry, and so on. Not only will they have access to these images, but they will also be able to research them, finding out about the artist, time period, country of origin, and so on. They'll be able to look to these images for inspiration, or they may get their inspiration from new imagery, computer images, and multimedia works.

Certainly, a number of questions can be raised about viewing art images on the computer screen, whether from CD-ROM or the Web. Such issues were once raised regarding reproductions, particularly slides, and most of us would agree that nothing can replace the experience of seeing an art image firsthand. But if that is not possible, the Web, CD-ROMs, and reproductions at least give us something near the real thing. With CD-ROMs, we can zoom into areas of a work for further study or pull back from it and reposition it with another work for comparison. The student can do these things with ease and can control his or her own learning. Learning does not have to be teacher-driven.

Although there is change in the industry, for now and for some time to come, multimedia is multimedia. Whether we discuss CD-ROM, DVD, or the Web, the creation of multimedia is the same—only storage and distribution are different. This may affect content, but, for now, the design of multimedia is the same, regardless of the format you use to display it.

None of this is perfect . . . not yet. The image is still small, and mass quantities of memory are needed for use and storage; creating a project takes a great deal of time; and although a multimedia creation may be different from anything else you've ever done, it is something to start thinking about. You may not get to

it right away. School budgets may be too tight to get you all the state-of-the-art equipment you'd like to have, but that's OK. However, when budget time comes up or when the school or district is thinking about buying new equipment, be ready to get your two cents in.

All the possibilities are both exciting and frightening. *Using* a CD-ROM for reference is easy. Creating your own is somewhat difficult, but possible. And more than that, it can be a fun, educational, and a rewarding experience for you and your students. The technology changes so quickly that it's next to impossible to keep up. Don't be afraid to ask questions. Perhaps let your students become your teacher. But most important: *don't panic!*

THE INTERNET: THE WORLD COMES TO THE ARTROOM

We are an information society: we move vast amounts of information across great distances. But the irony is that we need more access, more "highway," and more space on those roads. The information is not just text, but also images (both still and moving) and sound (live, recorded, spoken, and sung). And not only does this information have to travel; it also has to travel fast—and far.

What we now have available to us is a virtual library of millions of books, journals, magazines, proceedings, papers, and human resources. Again, this is not just textual information. There are virtually hundreds of galleries, museums, libraries, and collections that provide access to images and research, formal and informal writings and studies, and magazine and newspaper articles and reports—and all of this is possible through the Internet. But best of all, anyone with a connection can access the information.

The Internet is also about *ideas*—the sharing, stimulation, and nurturing of ideas—and it is about research without boundaries. These ideas come in all shapes and sizes; from people of all ages, colors, and

Brian Miner
Wrinkles of the World, *Photoshop*
Union High School, Union, MO

Corry Bulkley
Clarisworks Paint
Tokeneke School, Darien, CT

creeds; from countries all over the world. The Internet is information unlimited. Connecting over fifty million people worldwide, the Internet grows daily, and estimates are that it will reach over 200 million people by the year 2000.

The Internet is a huge network that links thousands of smaller computer networks and individual computers throughout the world. With the Internet, you can communicate with people anywhere in the world; access information, regardless of where it is located; and use all this for yourself or with your students. The Internet provides access to information through remote log-on, file transfer, and e-mail.

You can communicate with e-mail; download entire programs, files, and data for personal or classroom use; browse through museums and libraries; access databases; read a newspaper from 1,000 miles away; listen to "lectures"; and chat with famous personalities or experts in a field. You can join discussion groups on topics ranging from aardvarks and art to zoology and zygotes. You can "cruise" the Internet to find artworks, artists who work in a particular medium, photographers, museum and gallery curators, cartoonists, the animators from Warner Brothers or Disney, filmmakers, writers, poets, singers, and songwriters . . . ad infinitum!

The Internet is about *ideas,* and we've only begun to explore the possibilities.

What the Internet Brings to Art Education

* An integration of knowledge. The Web combines text with still and motion graphics and sound. Using hypermedia access, students can follow their own instincts when surfing the Net.
* Collaborative learning. Students can work with classmates or with students from the other side of the district to the other side of the world to inquire about alternative approaches to studying art, to collaborate on art images, and to develop other creative projects.
* True multicultural studies—connections with people, places and things. Write to anyone, anywhere. Talk to anyone, anywhere; and even see anyone, anywhere, anytime. All this can combine for a wonderful exploration into the study of art, art history, and aesthetics with people from all over the world. Set up a "chat," or e-mail students from other parts of the world. Set up a discussion group, or just toss out some questions for consideration. Think of the possibilities of your students' entering into a real discussion of the work of the Impressionists with students in France; or of their exploring the work of the Inuit and chatting with Inuit students their own age!

Marc T. Esguerra
F. M. Gaudineer Middle School,
Springfield, NJ

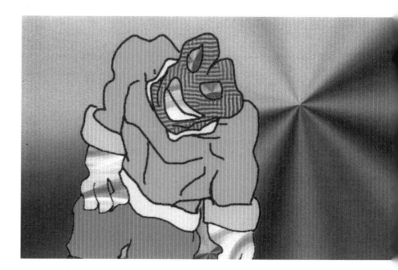

• Different learners, different styles. Because the Web combines so many different resources and displays them in so many different ways, it can appeal to a variety of learning personalities, more than any teacher could in a class period. Moreover, because so many students have Web access at home, they can continue this sort of exploration after school hours.

• Images, sounds, documents, and even movies from a variety of sources. You can go to a variety of sites, such as the National Gallery of Art, the Smithsonian, the Metropolitan Museum of Art, the Getty Foundation, the Louvre, or the Vatican. Go to an artist's studio or an art classroom from another part of the country.

• Research, research, research. Students can look up artists or images or information from museums, galleries, and libraries worldwide.

And this is just the start. As you and your students get more familiar with what the Web offers, and as speed and access are improved, there's no telling how much further you'll be able to push the technology to advance your art curriculum.

A Look at the Internet

There are two reasons that this will not be a definitive look at the Internet. First, there are books about the Internet that are hundreds of pages long, and there are shelves and shelves of these books. Some are *Accessing the Internet, Using the Web, A Complete Guide to Resources on the Web,* and *The Internet for Dummies* (one of my favorites). There are also books about creating homepages, creating and managing Web sites, selling on the Web, and the Web and education. This is just a starting point, a brief overview to get you interested in what all the hype is about and some hints on using the Web in your art curriculum.

The second reason that this cannot be the definitive look is that the Internet is a constantly changing "place." Some Web sites and homepages change daily, and that ability to adapt and change is one of the more exciting aspects of the Web. While this is a wonderful advantage when looking up information (you can actually "see" news stories as they happen), it can be terribly frustrating when explaining the

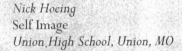

Nick Hoeing
Self Image
Union High School, Union, MO

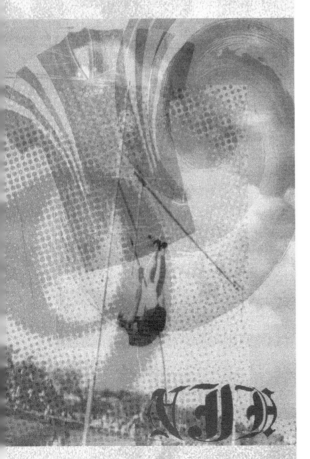

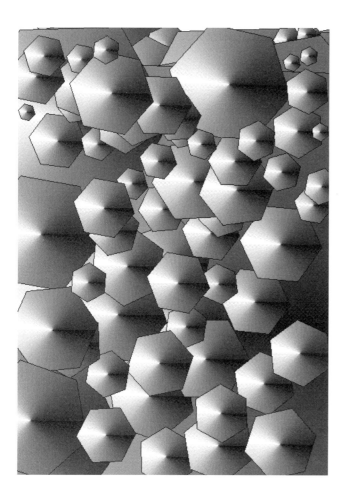

Chris Manna
BW Shapes
*High Mountain Road School, Franklin
Lakes, NJ*

Web to new users. I can't be sure that the information I give you today about a particular Web site will be true tomorrow! But this frustration is a small price to pay for the ideas and information that live on the Internet.

So, here is a start. Once you begin to see all you can do with Internet access and all the things your students can do on the Web, you'll be convinced of its value as an educational tool and resource. Remember: if you're a "newbie," *be patient, and don't panic!*

A Brief History of the Internet

The Internet began in the late sixties as ARPANET, a network that let users share software and hardware resources within the Advanced Research Projects Agency (ARPA) at the Department of Defense. ARPANET was initially used to link researchers with remote computer centers, allowing them to share resources such as databases and disk space. In the early years, access was the domain of military defense, but grew to academia and the academic research community. In the late 1970s, several other cooperative networks, such as USENET (Users' Network), came into being. In the early 1980s, Computer Science Network (CSNET) and BITNET arrived. These networks began providing nationwide networking to universities and research communities. These were not, however, part of the Internet.

The NSFNET (National Science Foundation Network), founded in 1986 to link university researchers throughout the United States, eventually expanded to connect the midlevel and statewide academic networks that connected universities and small research centers. This was possible because of the development of an operating system from UNIX that was offered to universities for practically nothing. UNIX made the connections easy, and soon everyone with a workstation had access.

NSFNET began replacing ARPANET; and in 1990, ARPANET was honorably discharged. Research centers in other countries then established new links with the Internet. The Internet now embraces over 50 million people on all seven continents. Factors key to the rapid growth of the Internet were the support of the government in the early nineties, the development of cheaper servers, on-line service providers for home use (such as America Online), HTML (the language that enables users to create Web pages), and Web browsers (which help users surf the Web easily).

How the Internet Works

The Internet, the worldwide supernetwork (actually a network of networks), is made up of thousands of independent computers in schools and universities (their address ends in .edu) and research centers (**.edu** or **.mil**), government agencies (**.gov**), and commercial enterprises (**.com**). Through the Internet, you can download files of information, gather in a newsgroup to share information or ideas, send e-mail, or even chat in real time with other users who are on-line.

When people talk about the Internet, they usually are referring to what they can do on the Internet. Some of the possibilities you will find are:

- **E-mail.** Exchange information with family, friends, students, people you don't know, people you may never meet—from all over the world: A mail list (listserv) allows you to subscribe to a list of people of like interest(s). When you mail something out, it goes to everyone on that list.

- **The Web.** The World Wide Web is the Internet, but with a structure called a graphical user interface (GUI). The Web uses a graphics-rich hypermedia interface of the Internet, which allows you to move from site to site with the click of a button. The resources include graphics, sound, full-motion video clips, and real-time video and sound (you can receive radio broadcasts over the Web).

- **Information retrieval.** You can retrieve information—text, graphics, images, movie clips, music—anywhere you go on the Internet. Visit the Metropolitan Museum of Art or the Louvre; go to a gallery and look at an artist's work; take a virtual reality tour of an architect's work. If your timing is right, you might even be able to set up a chat with an artist.

- **Chat rooms**. Although most chat rooms are really gossip areas, many writers and artists do make themselves available so that you can enter a chat area and have a (typed) conversation with them!

- **Shopping.** Yes, you can do all your holiday shopping on-line! Order books, bikes, brushes, paints, pandas, or pictures. Send cards or flowers. You can even buy hardware and software.

- **Newsgroups.** These are on-line "bulletin boards" set up by people of like interests. Unlike e-mail, these bulletin boards contain "public postings" that anyone can access and make comments on. All of this is for anyone who accesses the newsgroup. These groups can offer interesting information, although they can also get bogged down in mindless chatter (like that in some chat rooms and like much conversation!). Newsgroups, around since the 1970s, are being replaced by other Internet services, including those offered by Internet providers and specific Web sites.

- **Games.** Games on the Internet are a popular pastime, particularly for young people who have grown tired of the CD-ROM games they mastered one week after receiving them. Moreover, the Web offers something more exciting and challenging than Nintendo or Sega: on the Web, you can actually play against someone—from anywhere in the world!

Kylie Winkleblack
High Mountain Road School, Franklin
Lakes, NJ

More on E-mail

E-mail is faster than the post office or overnight mail, and less formal. E-mail has fostered a new method of communication. It's not merely point to point; it allows for mass communication as well. In other words, I can e-mail you, or a student, or a colleague, *or* I can send the same message to all three of you.

The ability to communicate immediately with anyone who has an e-mail address is really a sort of revolution; it has changed the way I communicate, not only with my students, but also with colleagues around the country.

- Because e-mail does not intrude (as a phone call can) on the person to whom you are sending it, people will likely send e-mail more readily. My students e-mail me regularly, sometimes with valid questions, sometimes with a clarification of an assignment, sometimes just to "chat." Students would never phone me at home, and would rarely write. Because I pick up my e-mail when it's convenient for me, it is less of an invasion on my time.

- People tend to answer their e-mail. If I'm sitting at my computer and am reading my e-mail, I tend to answer the mail as soon as I read it. Sometimes, it's just an acknowledgment of the note, but even just that will let the sender know that I've gotten his or her message.

- E-mail is less formal than regular mail. We tend to overlook spelling or grammar errors in e-mail. Educators may not consider this to be a good thing, but it does make the process of writing, especially to an instructor, less daunting.

- Because e-mail is informal, you might find that you write to more people more regularly. Sometimes, you'll send just a note; sometimes, a photo; sometimes, a full-length letter.

- An e-mailer can create a mailing list (often referred to as a "listserv") and communicate with small groups of people at a time. As a subscriber to a mailing list, you get e-mail from the group (usually composed of members with a similar interest), and you can send e-mail to everyone in the group, which can include quite a number of people. If you subscribe to too many, you can find yourself inundated with e-mail. I use mailing lists with my classes. For example, if I need to get a message to my stu-

THE WORLD WIDE WEB I know that teachers are using the Web in their classes at all levels, from K to grade 12. Here are some suggestions for using the Web:

- Have students use the Web to research an artist or period of art.

- Have students get in touch with students from other parts of the country—or world!—and discuss art activities they are doing, works they have seen, and museums they visited.

- Have students post images on the Web.

- Have students explore galleries.

- Have students work on collaborative activities with students from other places.

Justin Meeks
J-Bot 2000, *Painter 5.0*
George Washington High School,
Danville, VA

Vanessa Romanoff
Cadillac Mountain, *Watercolor enhanced in Photopaint*
Falmouth Middle School, Falmouth, ME

dents before the next class, I can contact all of them on the mailing list by writing just one e-mail and sending it to "all." I might come across something in the newspaper or the TV listing that I won't be able to inform students of, or I might clarify an assignment I gave in class.

Besides the Web and e-mail, you could use FTP (file-transfer protocol), which makes accessible thousands of pieces of information you would never have read or seen. You can download a discussion with other art teachers on a topic you've selected, an article someone has suggested you read, or a paper or proceedings from a conference. Students can research in libraries they've never heard of and museums they've never seen.

Telnet is a communications protocol that lets you log on to a host computer and use its resources. Thus, the Mac or IBM in your classroom connects to a remote site, allowing you to access information not only from a library in your town or state, but also from libraries (college, university, or research libraries) across the country and throughout the world.

Getting Connected

Now for the physical connections. You will need:

Access

For a computer at school, your computer or technology coordinator can tell you how to get onto the Internet. However, if you are trying to get started at home, you can sign up with an on-line service or an Internet-only provider.

Before you sign up, know the modem speed (14.4K, 28.8K, 33.6K, or 56K), and ask if local numbers are available at the faster speeds. When I upgraded to a 56 K modem, I found that I could not access the higher-speed connection by a local phone call: I had to use a toll number. The speed of the modem didn't seem quite so important then, considering the increased cost. There's no need to spend money on a 56 K modem if your provider doesn't have a local access number available at that speed. Make sure that whatever you choose is cost-effective, based on your use of the Internet. Note that some providers do not have the ability, as of this writing, to allow you to take advantage of the faster modems. However, you might be able to get an ISDN, 56K, or T1 line; and in some areas, your cable company can provide Internet access either with a connection directly to your computer or through Web TV.

Modem

A modem modulates information—usually originating from a computer or fax machine—so that it can travel across the phone lines. When it arrives at your computer, it gets "modulated" again (or demodulated) so that your computer can "read" it (modulated-demodulated = "modem").

Most new computers come with a built-in modem. As of this writing, the highest baud rate (or speed at which the information travels) available is 56K. However, 28.8K is fine! Besides, the processing speed (MHz) of your computer is also important, especially when working on the Web.

Software

Finally, you need some kind of communications software so that you can "talk" to your modem. Many modems come packaged with software, but you might already have communications software with another package (such as ClarisWorks). Or you may want to use an on-line service provider like America Online (AOL).

On-line Services

You really don't need to know all the technical terminology, but you do want to get the fastest and most reliable and cost-effective service you can find. The biggies were once CompuServe, AOL, and Prodigy. Now, America Online is the largest, having bought out CompuServe, but there are so many other providers getting into the thick of it that it's hard to make a call as to what will be the best way to go in the near future. Cable companies and local telephone companies are now getting into the business of providing on-line service. They promise to be faster than using regular phone lines, but their service may cost a bit more.

An on-line service's interface is very easy to use. E-mail is right there when you log on, and there is technical support ("support" is a relative term: I have been more aggravated than helped on many occasions, but the result can sometimes be worth the wait).

Internet-only service providers (such as RCN, Netcom, and AT&T) are growing in number and in service provided. Because the industry is changing so rapidly, a list of these providers would quickly become dated. For a good overview of what's available in your area, try www.thelist.com for a list of Internet providers by state/region. If you go on trips or a vacation of any length, you might also want to check here for access providers.

After installing the software from the provider, click on the program icon. It will prompt you to enter your name and password. Once you log on, you will be brought to a main screen with options offering you shopping, mail service, Internet access, chat rooms, and other special areas that the service provides. From here on, you need to experiment and get used to how the service works and what it offers.

Many people who initially used an on-line service later opted for an Internet provider. On-line services can grow tiresome, and if what you are using mostly is the Internet, you may be paying for services you don't use. (An Internet provider does provide e-mail accounts.)

Michelle Hoffman
Photoshop
Randolph High School, Morristown, NJ

Eric Decter
Pooches
F. M. Gaudineer Middle School, Springfield, NJ

How the Web Works

The hypertext markup language (HTML) of the Web operates much like HyperCard or HyperStudio, giving you a graphical interface to access information by *linking* you to other sources (or pages).

You probably know that www refers to World Wide Web, but what's a URL? A URL (uniform resource locator) is the address of a Web site. For example, in the URL http://www.whitehouse.gov

- **http** refers to hypertext transfer protocol and is the language used by the Web. Beginning the URL with http indicates that this is a Web page (http://www) and not a file (ftp://) or a gopher site (gopher://).
- **//** indicates that the information that follows is the name of the machine or place you will be accessing
- **www** refers to the World Wide Web
- **whitehouse** is the name of the site
- **.gov** means that this is a government site

The type of site is indicated by a period and the last three letters. Each country also has an address and the initials used are often self-explanatory. For example, .uk stands for the United Kingdom and .fr stands for France.

Kristen Faber
High Mountain Road School, Franklin
Lakes, NJ

Last three letters	URL	Brings you to this site
.gov = government	www.ed.gov	U.S. Department of Education
.edu = education	www.stjohns.edu	St. John's University, New York and Rome
.org = organization	www.metmuseum.org	Metropolitan Museum of Art
.com = commercial	www.microsoft.com	Microsoft Corporation

A Web Browser: Do I Need One?

A Web browser simply guides you through the Web; and, yes, you do need one. Among others are Netscape and Microsoft's Internet Explorer. An on-line service (like AOL) will provide you with a browser, as will most Internet providers.

The major commands (buttons) you will see on the browser will include:

- **the URL,** or address area
- **Back:** allows you to go to a previous page
- **Forward:** allows you to go to a page forward from where you are; you have to go back before you can go forward
- **Stop:** allows you to stop if accessing a site seems to be taking forever
- **Reload:** allows you to try a busy site again if it is unavailable. When you try again, you use the reload button instead of the enter command when you select the URL.

Bookmarks, Hot Lists, Favorite Places: probably included with your browser, a function (known by any of these three names) that allows you to keep a permanent list of Web sites you have visited and want to revisit. Therefore, you do not need to memorize or keep a URL hard-copy list of the sites you want to revisit. Students might like to save the sites of schools they have visited and with whom they may wish to work in the future. (If you are wise, you will make a backup file of your bookmarks so you can retrieve them in the event of a hard-drive crash.)

You see, things really do get easier!

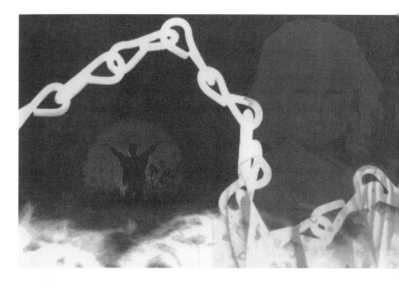

Melissa Rhodes
Arts High School, Minnesota Center for
Arts Education, Golden Valley, MN

Search Engines

In the June 1996 issue of *MacUser,* search engines were referred to as the "hunter-gatherers of the Net...plumbing their own databases and others around the world, returning lists of Web pages, FTP sites, and even USENET messages that contain the keywords you've entered." That hunter-gatherer reference is really accurate. If you want to find anything (and I do mean anything) on the Net, use a search engine. There are many including WebCrawler, excite, AltaVista, Lycos, Magellen and HotBot.

Wendy Bryant
Photogenics
George Washington High School,
Danville, VA

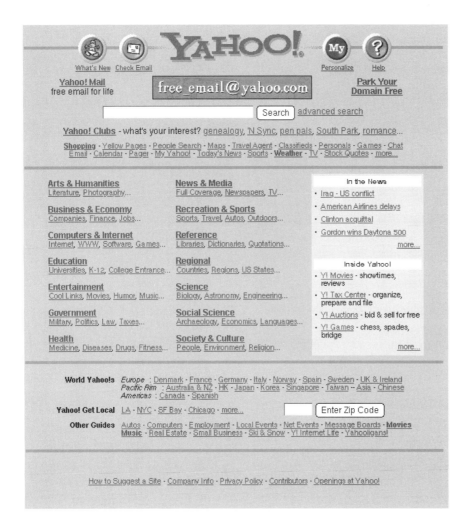

Yahoo! is a directory service that provides the user with a friendly search engine as well. These screen images illustrate what happens when you go to www.yahoo.com. The first directory lists the many areas you can go to in Yahoo like Arts and Humanities, Education, Entertainment, etc. From here you can also conduct a search. If you click on Arts and Humanities, Yahoo will bring you to the Arts and Humanities directory (www.yahoo.com/Arts); from here you can either do a search or go to a subdirectory like Art History, Entertainment, Education, etc. Clicking on Education will bring you to the third screen (www.yahoo.com/Arts/Education) where you can again either do a search or check the subdirectory that Yahoo offers.

Reproduced with permission of Yahoo! Inc. ©1998 by Yahoo! Inc. Yahoo! and the YAHOO! logo are trademarks of YAHOO! Inc.

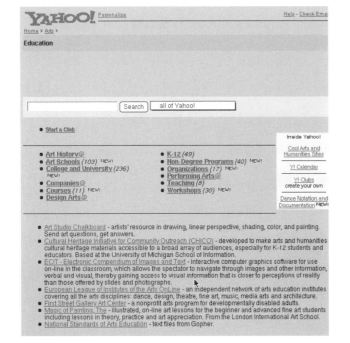

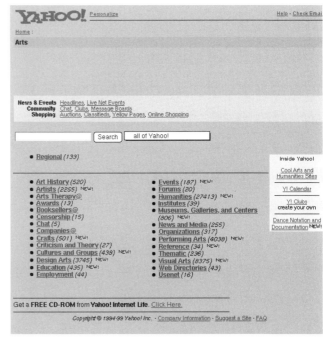

GREAT WEB SITES When I work with teachers on using the Web for the first time, they tell me that the thought of remembering all the letters and symbols that go into a URL can be just a bit daunting. To make this easier, I suggest that they remember just two Web addresses. I have selected these because of the quality and quantity of Web links they provide. (For some wonderful Web sites for art teachers and students, see page 136.)

http://www.artsednet.getty.edu is The Getty Center: ArtsEdNet site. (From here, you can get to almost any gallery or museum, to lots of art-education resources, and to ArtsEdNetTalk, a mailing list of art educators.)

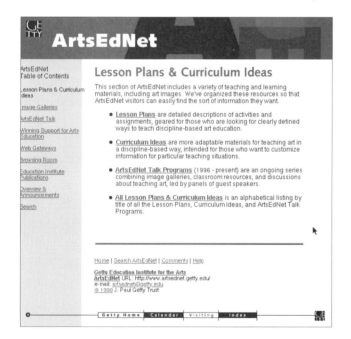

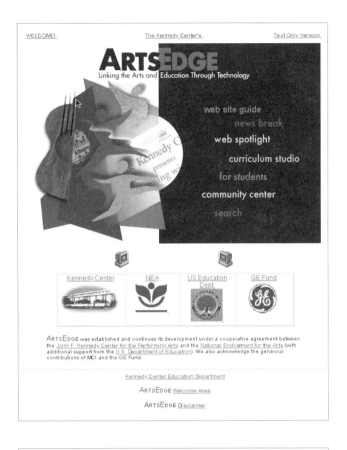

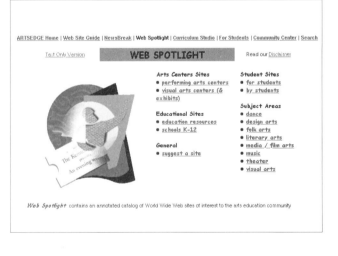

http://artsedge.kennedy-center.org is The Kennedy Center: ArtsEdge site. (Note that there is no www for this site. From here, you can get to a myriad of museums, galleries, resources, educational sites, and Web links. Also take a look at the wonderful homepage of The Kennedy Center: http://www.kennedy-center.org. (But don't type in that last period—it's only for the end of the sentence here!)

Creating for the Web

"What is a homepage, and can I have one? Can I have a Web site?"

Yes, and yes. If you would like to put your school or your art program on the Web, discuss the technical requirements with your computer coordinator. If you are doing this personally from home, discuss it with your Internet provider. There are several programs that can help you do this, including Claris's HomePage, Adobe's PageMill, FrontPage, and even PageMaker. A few years ago, the only way to publish on the Web was by using HTML (hypertext markup language), but these software packages allow easy design without programming knowledge or knowledge of HTML. Therefore, Web pages are not hard for you or your students to create. However, remember basic design principles!

Have your students surf the Web to visit sites from a variety of sources and to look at them with a critical eye. Below are some questions and advice that you might have students consider.

* Do the sites capture your interest? Is the layout inviting?
  Advice (when creating your own site): Remember design principles!
* Are graphics used? Do the graphics download in a timely fashion, or do they seem to take forever? Are images clear?
  Advice: Be selective in the quality and number of images you use.
* Is the text easy to read?
  Advice: Use a serif font for large blocks of text. Times, Times Roman, and Palatino are good choices.
* Is there enough information? Too much information?
  Advice: Be sure of what you want to say, and write it out before you "publish" it.
* How is color used?
  Advice: Colors that look good in print may not look good on-screen. This is especially true when using color combinations and when printing text over a background color or image.

These questions will get you started. If you and your students are going to design Web pages, design them well. Work with students on layout and the use of graphics, color and text. A few points to consider are:

* the image area to use to create the page if there are several different monitor sizes in use
  Advice: You'll be safe if you design for a 15" monitor.
* Web browsers' formats for displaying information
  Advice: On your Web page, put a note that advises the visitor what browser your site looks best on (for example: "This site works best in Netscape").
* slow download of graphics
  Advice: As wonderful as graphic images are, you have to remember that graphics take up time and disk space. This is important especially if students are doing a lot of their work at home, where Internet access may be slower than at school or a library.

Several books listed in Part Six will help you with design problems you might encounter with the Web; the "For Dummies" series is always a good choice! Remember: you are the art teacher. *Teach art!*

BRINGING TECHNOLOGY INTO THE CLASSROOM

PART FOUR

Entering into a discussion on curriculum guidelines is no easy task. Each state has its own department of education, divided by county, district, or locality. Advice on how to develop a curriculum, then, is only that—advice. No one can predict how something will work in a given situation. You know yourself that even though a lesson works with one class, it can fall right on its face with another. Here are some strategies to consider.

- **Look at your program.**

You are the person who best knows your teaching situation: the school and/or curriculum philosophy; the background of your students; the constraints you have to work around, including class size, classroom size, and number of meetings per week or semester. You are the only person responsible for the successful use of computers within your curriculum, and you are the only one who can ensure their successful, artistic use. Don't be pushed into something you're not ready for, but do get ready for computers!

- **Know your students.**

Know your students, and plan your program in relation to the total school curriculum. What does the art department want students to know, and when do they want them to know it? Do students come from homes with computers? Are they using computers in other subject areas? How much time is given to computers in other areas? Are computers available to art students at upper levels? Can you assume students come to you with a knowledge of computers? For instance, are students given computer lessons in the first or second grade by their classroom teacher or a computer teacher?

- **Think of long-term planning.**

You may decide not to use computers in K–3, waiting instead until the fourth or fifth grade. There is really no age guideline. Very young children enjoy the computer, and are especially good with it if they have one at home. Talk to other teachers so that you can get a sense of what level you feel computers should be introduced. Look at this as a program that builds, with computers as just a part of that total plan.

Approach the planning of computer use as you would any other large piece of equipment (like a potter's wheel or printing press). Consider demonstrating a tool or technique and then having students work individually or in small groups on the computer, in a rotation method. In elementary education particularly, think of incorporating technology over the long-term K–6 school experience rather than at each grade level.

- **Space: there's never enough!**

No one has enough space in his or her artroom, so keeping the computers in the classroom demands a bit of interior design. You can plan a solid program around one or two computers, but, of course, four or five are better! Many art teachers have set aside a corner of the artroom; others have one or two on carts that they can roll into a closet when they are not in use. Of course, if they are not out all the time, will students think of using them?

Use a computer classroom or lab if you want the whole class to work on a project at the same time. For instance, if you were working on a project with a time limit, having the whole class work for two to three periods in a lab would be much quicker than having them work in small groups at two or three computers in your clasroom. Some teachers have also found that working in a lab quickly reinforces software tools that you denomstrate to a class. So, for example, if you were showing students how to use PhotoDeluxe or Painter Classic, having them all go to a lab to work with the software would reinforce the tools you demonstrated in class.

Although you needn't be overly cautious about the computer, dust and dirt can cause damage. Because they work in clay and metals, high-school students seem to generate more of the harmful dust. Heavy dust and filings can be deadly. Take care of the computers, and keep them covered when not in use.

- **Time: there's never enough!**

Time spent working on computers has to be based on how often you meet students. If you meet students only once a week for half a year, it wouldn't make sense to spend seven or eight weeks using computers.

Jessica Cotton
Arts High School, Minnesota Center
for Arts Education, Golden Valley, MN

If you have a unified program, however, it's more reasonable to think that in the course of grades 1–3, students will have spent several hours of class time on the computer. You can assume some basic skills: students will know how to turn on the computer, open and save files, and print out images. They will have a basic control of input devices and familiarity with available software, and of the tools available within the software used.

•   **Equipment: there's never enough!**

In Guidelines for Combining Technology and the Artroom (page 12), I suggest you go on a fact-finding mission to explore what equipment your school already has. Find out what's available in terms of money and equipment, and what computers are already in school. Use whatever platform—Macs or Windows—that your school has. Besides, within the next five to ten years, all computers and software will likely be compatible and interchangeable. You'll want a color printer (a color ink-jet printer would be fine). Find out if your school has a laser printer or a scanner that you can use. A scanner is great, but if you use it for only the occasional lesson or project, you don't need one in the artroom all the time. Having a laser printer is also great, but if you have only enough money for one printer, make it a color printer. How many computers should you have in the artroom? It all depends on you, your curriculum, and the room you're using. However, you do not need top-of-the-line equipment. (See Part Eight.)

•   **Use the equipment, and you'll get more.**

Of course, this is not always true. But if you show an interest in using computers and computer-related technologies in your art program, you'll have a far better chance of upgrading your equipment (or getting some in the first place) than if you grumble and moan about not having equipment or complain about having to learn how to use it.

•   **Demonstrate.**

Demonstrate software or a lesson using a large-screen monitor, video projector, or an LCD panel (a device that connects the computer monitor to an overhead projector). This equipment is expensive. If you have to make use of the computer and monitor (usually a 15" monitor), you might want to have students gather around the computer in small groups and give the demonstration two or three times.

Elisabeth Cordner
Clarisworks Paint
Tokeneke School, Darien, CT

• **Explore.**
Work on computers is collaborative. (For a few suggestions, see "Multimedia in the Artroom," on page 17.) Think of group projects that allow students to use a variety of talents and more than just computers. Have students combine sound and music with still and moving images. Have them work in traditional media and "mix" them with computer-created images. When you discuss aesthetics, art history, and criticism, encourage students to explore a variety of resources—including the World Wide Web—for research.

In ten to fifteen years, students may be coming to school with a computer in their backpack. But right now, the reality is that some of you do not have a computer in your artroom; many of you have only one or two computers; and some fortunate few have several and have access to a lab. Use your best classroom-management skills to plan how to use whatever equipment you have, just as you would a potter's wheel, loom, or printing device.

When equipment is limited, most teachers rotate or work students in groups. In elementary education particularly, think of incorporating technology over the long-term K–6 experience, rather than at each grade level; or try to get into a computer lab so that the whole class can have a simultaneous computer experience. Although similar suggestions apply to middle schools, things shift in high school.

In the upper grades, depending on your curriculum, you might want to introduce computers in one of two ways. You might develop a computer-art or computer-graphics course for which you have lab access and can have students explore design, drawing, or some area of the graphic arts or desktop publishing. Or, you might incorporate computers into your total curriculum. For instance, for a studio project, offer students the opportunity to work on computers. If students are working with text, suggest that they manipulate it on the computer. When studying the work of artists, have students look at artworks created by computers, as well as those created in traditional media. Suggest to students that they use the computer, particularly the Web, for research when preparing a paper or presentation discussing art history, criticism, and aesthetics.

Remember, too, to look to the various alternative resources available with computer technologies, like the variety of CD-ROM titles and the World Wide Web. Students at every level can use these resources, if they are available.

Jennifer Yoo
Photoshop
Randolph High School, Morristown, NJ

THE IDEAL: WHAT A MODEL ARTROOM MIGHT BE

Elementary school. For an elementary-school class of twenty-five to thirty students, you have two or three computers plus a large-screen monitor or LCD panel for demonstration purposes. All computers have access to the Internet. You have one color printer, a scanner, and external storage. For software, you have Kid Works and some other versatile program, such as ClarisWorks; for graphics, Kid Pix and Art Dabbler; for image editing, Soap or Color it! or PhotoDeluxe.

Middle school. For a middle-school class, you have three to five computers and a teacher's station with a large-screen monitor for demonstration. Besides a versatile program (like ClarisWorks) and graphics programs (like Kid Pix, Art Dabbler, and Painter Classic), you have more sophisticated programs (PageMaker and CorelDRAW), a presentation package (HyperStudio or PowerPoint), and an imaging package (Soap, Color it!, PhotoDeluxe, or even Photoshop). You also have Web-design software (PageMill or Claris' Home Page), a scanner, a digital camera, and, perhaps, a camcorder.

High school. Your high-school art studio resembles a state-of-the-art graphics studio. Technology is used not just in computer-specific courses, but is available for all courses. If the following equipment is not in the graphics lab, it is available in some other art area.

- Twenty to twenty-five of the newest, fastest, most powerful computers—all with the largest hard drives, vast quantities of memory, modem, CD-ROM drive, 19" and 21" monitors, graphic tablets . . . Remember: this is the ideal!
- A scanner and printer for every five to ten machines; two black-and-white laser printers, two ink-jet printers, and a quality thermal or laser color printer that prints 11" x 17"; video equipment that includes a video workstation, a rewritable CD-R drive to "write" CD-ROMs, and, of course, Internet access all around.

- The latest versions of software that are comparable to (but by the time you read this, better than) Illustrator, PageMaker, Quark, Director, Premier, Painter, CorelDRAW, Sound Editor, PowerPoint, and Persuasion; Web software; animation and 3-D rendering software. The software is updated regularly, and there is no budget limitation.

Each of the other "traditional" art studios has five or six computers equipped as above. Students are encouraged to use computers when and if the spirit moves them—for painting, photography, design, drawing, filmmaking, video, and multimedia. All student portfolios exist on some sort of removable storage (Zip or Jaz disks or CD-ROM). All of the screens are visible at the same time, which allows you and the students to see images emerge.

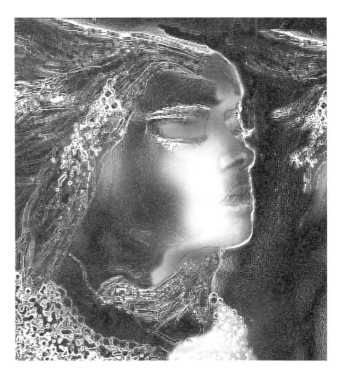

Rachel Saak
My Face
Homewood-Flossmoor High School, Flossmoor, IL

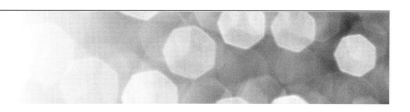

THE REALITY

The reality of the situation is that you might have one computer in your artroom, and you might have access to a lab. Further, budgets are never unlimited; computers are never updated regularly; and you have no time for training. So, how do you deal with the reality?

When computers were first put into schools, the computer lab was the preferred way to go. Times have changed, and what most educators now realize is that if the computer isn't in the room, teachers and students aren't going to use it for assignments. Some schools have upgraded the lab equipment, putting the old equipment into the classroom; other schools have gotten a computer for every teacher or classroom.

If you have a computer lab, use it. Although there are some schools in which a few departments or teachers monopolize the lab, that may be because they were interested in using it long before you were. They got first shot at the lab because they were first out of the gate, so to speak. But it's time you got your share. See if you can get the lab for one grade level each month, for two art periods.

Ask your colleagues if you can borrow a computer or two for a brief time for a special project. You might be able to bring the number of computers in your classroom up to five for a week or two.

Suggest that several "extra" computers be purchased for your school and be put on carts so that they can be wheeled from classroom to classroom as teachers need them. You would borrow these not unlike you would borrow AV equipment from the media specialist.

If you haven't got a large-screen monitor in your classroom, ask your technology coordinator if there is an LCD panel (it attaches to an overhead projector). You'll want to have some sort of large screen that students can see while you demonstrate a piece of software or a CD-ROM. Giving students a demonstration of a project on the computer gives them the information they need to get started on a project on their own or in a small group.

Peter Reilly
Clarisworks Paint
Tokeneke School, Darien, CT

If you feel uncomfortable with the graphics packages you have, start by showing one or two CD-ROMs to students. Then have them work in small groups. For example, if your school has *Encarta* or some other encyclopedia on CD-ROM, show students how to start the CD-ROM and how to search through it. Then give them an assignment. This could be something as simple as getting information on an artist or a period of art history. They can use this information to write a report or as part of an alternative project. If you have access to the Internet, your students can enter into a discussion about their favorite artist or painting with students from other schools. They could even share their own works on the Web.

All of this is a very optimistic look at technology in art education. The reality is that you are lucky if you have one computer in your clasroom. And if it's a Mac or a computer with Windows 95, you are really lucky. Again, the reality is that the elementary classroom often gets hand-me-downs from the high school, which is used equipment that will not run the latest versions of graphics programs and may not have a CD-ROM drive.

The point is that you can use one computer in your classroom very effectively, whether for the making of art or for research about art. You can give assignments that can be done in rotation, and students can take turns. Remember: you are teaching art, not technology. Assignments on computer should flow from your art curriculum.

Software

The ideal would be to have every bit of software you need on all the computers in the school where you teach. No budget crunches, no technical difficulties. Whatever you want. That would also assume that you had the time and money to go for training in using all the software.

The software packages mentioned here are only suggestions for what you might consider, particularly if you are working on a budget. While none is the ultimate package for art teachers, they are all very good programs, reasonably priced, and designed for either the Mac or Windows platform. This means that no matter what computer platform students have at home, Mac or Windows, they can use the software you use in school.

Software changes rapidly, and although the titles cited in this book have been around for several years, it is possible that a publisher will discontinue a package or change it altogether. These recommendations are just a place to start. You may have found software you like better; you may not care for something suggested here. What really matters is that you find a package that you feel comfortable with—and that you use it!

For the Elementary School
Kid Pix can be used with any grade level; I even use it occasionally with my college students, just for a change. But it is best used in K–5. Kid Pix introduces students to all the basic icons they will find in more advanced programs. Steer the class away from all the bells and whistles that come with the program. Kid Pix Studio includes Moopies, Wacky TV, and Digital Puppets, which are cute, but not if you don't plan on

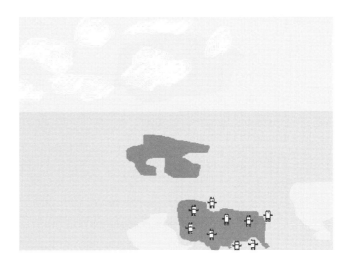

Alessandro Argenio
Clarisworks Paint
Tokeneke School, Darien, CT

using these elements in your curriculum. A teacher asked me recently, "How do you get them to use just the tools you want them to?" It is hard to limit them. It is sometimes helpful to give students a period of time to play around with all the options. They usually find the opportunity a bit overwhelming, and they welcome limitations.

Dabbler (or Art Dabbler) is advertised as a "natural" drawing tool, and it is different. I'm not sure it's as natural as a pen or pencil, but it clearly works more the way we do as artists. It readies students for more sophisticated programs, like Photoshop and Painter. The tools include marker, crayon, and chalk. Plus, the user can select and mix paper textures, and apply a number of effects to the image or part of the image. Dabbler works well with students in grades 2–8, and even into high school. I like it because it is different from Kid Pix and it offers a very different medium for computers.

ClarisWorks is used in most elementary and middle schools and, at one time, came preloaded on most Macs. Since your school probably has ClarisWorks, use it; it's a good program. Besides having word processing, database, and spreadsheet programs, ClarisWorks has both a draw and a paint program. It is important for students to learn the difference between the two, and ClarisWorks certainly fits the bill. It can be used well in grades 4–8 and higher.

If you want to teach your students image manipulation, Color it! or PhotoDeluxe or Soap will do the trick. A friend of mine refers to Color it! as "Photoshop for the rest of us." Some elementary teachers also use HyperStudio, Kid Works, Photoshop, and PROmotion in their curriculum. Use whatever you are comfortable with.

For the Middle School

You can further student use of all the programs suggested for the elementary school by incorporating the use of multimedia, as well expanding on programs like HyperStudio, Painter Classic, and PowerPoint. Some middle-school students are learning to produce student publications and use Student Writing Center, ClarisWorks, Microsoft Office, and even PageMaker. Don't forget that students, in addition to learning various software programs, should also be learning how to use scanners and digital cameras.

For the High School

See all the programs above!

High schools may or may not have a larger budget for buying software. High-school students can concentrate in areas such as graphic art, fine art, and photography. For these students, then, you have to know what they are preparing for: a career or college? Art major or not? Your curriculum is probably already geared to the students' direction. The following software is suggested because it is standard fare in the business world and higher education.

On all computers, you have access to PageMaker or Quark, Painter, Photoshop, Illustrator or Freehand, PowerPoint or Persuasion. (All of these are available for both Mac and Windows, usually at a decent lab-pack or site-licensing price.) On selected computers, 3-D rendering programs, HyperStudio, Director, and video-editing programs like Premier can be used. Sound editing, animation, and morphing are also great programs.

Please note: *don't panic!*

If your school cannot afford to buy all this software, or if you are working on a limited number of machines, or if your program is not strong in technology, or if you yourself don't feel comfortable with this software—*don't panic!* Most colleges and employers still assume that students have little experience with computers and/or graphics software. What they are most concerned with is their knowledge of the elements and principles of art. So, if your students do not get to use these programs before they graduate from high school, they'll manage. If students already have basic art skills—and something to say— they can easily learn to use Photoshop or Illustrator.

This sample screen from Dabbler illustrates the variety of tools featured in the tool drawer including pen, pencil, chalk, marker, crayon, spray can, eyedropper, and liquid brush. This menu of visual icons also features the fill, magnify, and rotate options. Cursor size choices are indicated by the triangles at lower right, and the star icons indicate options for treating selected areas of the image: scaling, moving, replacing, or applying special effects. For another screen view, see page 69. Dabbler image courtesy of MetaCreations.

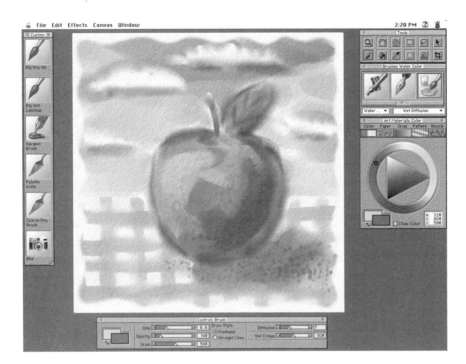

Painter Classic was developed by MetaCreations to provide users with a package that bridges the gap between the simple interface of Dabbler and the more powerful and complicated software package, Painter. Painter Classic simplifies the options available in Painter, but does not limit the possibilities that can be achieved. The interface is very similar to Painter, and you will note that "natural" tools are featured. So for example, students can choose from brushes, chalk, markers and pencils to create their work. Colors are selected from a color wheel rather than predefined "swatches" of color. There are a number of special effects available as well. Painter image courtesy of MetaCreations.

Classroom Strategies

As with any new medium, students will need an introductory demonstration on the operation of the computer and the use of software available to them. The possibility of using the computer lab for an introductory lesson or two was discussed in the previous section, as was the use of large screen monitors for demonstration purposes. Either of these suggestions will save you the time of having to instruct students individually or in small groups.

Limit your demonstrations to the care and handling of the computer, and the use of one or two pieces of software. Use the same methodologies you would use when introducing any art medium, such as pen and ink, clay, or weaving.

The software features and menu structures of most commercial software are quite similar. Options like draw, cut and paste, brush, shape commands, fill, and undo are found in most graphics software packages and dedicated graphics workstations, although they are considerably more refined. Students will recognize these similarities, and should be able to move quite easily among graphics software packages.

Limiting Options

When first assigning projects, limit the menu options students may choose from. An easy-to-use software package, particularly one recommended for elementary schools, makes a good starting point. The menu is simple to understand and has only fifteen or so options. Given a limited choice, students tend to explore more deeply. Such exploration helps students build a good foundation before they use the similar options in more sophisticated programs like Photoshop, Illustrator, Painter, and CorelDRAW.

Limiting choices also encourages the artistic process because students don't get sidetracked by more complicated commands. For example, when some students discover a special effect like the gradient fills or special brushes, they often use it to excess.

Further, art teachers who have used computers note that sometimes students feel overwhelmed by the vast array of options and colors found in sophisticated software and get easily discouraged, or find they do not have enough class time to master them. You want to give your students a good foundation.

Note: Remind students to save their work periodically. Not only will this allow you and your students to view the development of an image, but it will protect the loss of an image due to a power or system failure.

JUST FOR TEACHERS:
ADMINISTRATIVE PAPERWORK

Following is an overview of several areas where you might consider using computers for the paperwork and record keeping that accompanies the teaching of art. With databases, spreadsheets, and word processing software, you can use the computer for day-to-day and year-to-year tasks such as ordering supplies, keeping inventories, and updating audiovisual materials. Keeping these lists on disk will save many hours, as you simply update each previous list.

You can even create a database—of lessons, activities, periods in art, artists, and styles—for your use or for students to consult. There are a variety of software packages available, and your school may already own one. Consult your computer coordinator for advice on which system might best suit your needs. Ask questions of people who have been using computers. There is no need for you to do everything alone, and most school systems have resource people on staff who can offer advice.

Nicole Cirelli
Collage, *Photoshop*
Randolph High School, Morristown, NJ

Steve Ehrenkrantz
Photoshop
Randolph High School, Morristown, NJ

Supply Orders and Inventories

With a database, any list or series can be updated or revised quickly. Putting your inventory on a database will help end the drudgery of typing your supply lists each year; you need only add or delete those items unique to a particular year. AV equipment and supplies, books, and periodicals can be also be inventoried and updated.

Database information can be accessed in a variety of ways, depending on how you wish to set up your information (for instance, by subject, author, topic, or year). A spreadsheet can be used for ordering, allowing you to keep an ongoing record of costs. A budget can easily be determined and a supply order generated merely by entering or deleting the supplies needed in a given year.

Lesson Plans

Consider creating a database of lessons for individuals or classes. You might consider emergency lesson plans, activities for students who have been absent, or activities for students who finish projects early.

If you create a database of activities, and catalog them by grade, subject, medium, and/or curriculum concept, you can retrieve them easily. For example, students could access activities that are related to a topic they are interested in, or activities based on an artist or period in history.

With a word processor, you can save your curriculum, lesson plans, tests, outlines, and other items on disk. Text-editing features make updating and revisions easy; you can make yearly revisions to just those sections with changes, without having to retype entire curricula.

MISCELLANEOUS RESOURCES There are many businesses you may want to contact for donated equipment or services. Examples include:

- For printing special projects, try contacting a local printer or business that uses color printers to see if they would print out your students' art works.

- Contact industries for equipment that isn't outdated to you (you may not want old computers, but what about old printers or scanners?).

- Many schools are utilizing Channel One (see page 34) and have at their disposal a good deal of video equipment. See if you can share in its use.

- Another resource may be your cable outlet or provider for equipment or program access. When cable franchises for operation are negotiated, most communities come to an agreement with the cable company that schools/education have some access to their resources (equipment, airwaves, studios).

Chris Majette
Reality 5, Photoshop
Randolph High School, Morristown, NJ

COMPUTERS IN DESIGN

Ryan James Cianchette
CorelDRAW
Falmouth Middle School, Falmouth, ME

Playing with ideas, exploring alternatives, and push-ing and pulling images to achieve a variety of effects are essential activities in all areas of art, but especially in the study of design. Most artists and students find that experimentation on computers is simple and easy. Students rarely hesitate to play with on-screen images, because they can simply move or erase a design element that is not quite right, with no risk to a finished work.

If students save experimental images—not only the more successful ones—they can return to them later for more careful analysis and judgment. And they can save their works in steps or stages, allowing them and you to explore the decisions made in the creative development of an image.

Computers can also relieve the drudgery of the repetitive tasks in introductory courses. If one design is to provide the basis of an exploration of the elements and principles of design, for example, in doing a color study, the original can be called upon easily, without redrawing, and be used over and over again.

Strategies: Designing with the Computer

These strategies are introductory problems that you might present to students. The problems can be used within a computer art course, as part of a unit on design, or as an assignment for individual students working on a rotation.

Consider incorporating some of these ideas within a unit that deals more specifically with an artist or style of art where design is an objective. Or, per-haps offer the option of completing an assignment on the computer, rather than in traditional media like pen, pencil, and paint.

Computer designs are often exciting and vibrant. When students can play with a variety of alternatives in their designs—experimenting with placement, composition, color, and positive and negative space—they actually explore more design possibilities, solve more design problems, and make more decisions regarding the effects of shape and placement on com-position than they might with traditional media. The ability to play with designs without the risk of losing successful elements of an image allows students more freedom to explore possibilities until they reach some aesthetic conclusions.

Many of the menu features correspond to the design elements covered in introductory courses. You can therefore assign projects that correspond to and utilize these menu features. The activities suggested in Using Menu Options (page 62) are similar to those used with traditional media. You may use them as pre-sented or incorporate them into a larger unit based on them, an artist, or a style. What you might find, however, is that students work faster and create more designs than they would by using paper and pencil. More does not necessarily mean better, but perhaps the more practice that students have in creating designs, the better they will become at creating and evaluating them.

What about evaluating these computer-created images? There is no need to treat these images any differently than those done in traditional media. You and students must still look at technique, style, use of medium, and content. Remember: "art is what artists do." (Nam June Paik) Whatever methods and criteria you use for traditional works should hold true for these.

Using Menu Options: Lines and Shapes

So that students can explore specific menu options—such as frame, circle, and line—have them create a series of designs of geometric shapes. You might choose to make the activities that follow more specific to your needs. For example, have students keep all points of the lines or shapes on-screen. You may wish to instruct students to isolate all shapes, with none overlapping, or to have all shapes touch or overlap. Or you may want to tailor for the computer a project that students have previously done with traditional media.

Note

Encourage students to save in steps or stages of development, and to change the name of each image before saving; for example, "Lines 1," "Lines 2," "Lines 3," and so on.

- Line/Lines

Have students create several designs using only the line or lines command. They might experiment with

the direction of the line(s), vary the width of line(s) by selecting different brushes, place lines on parallel planes and/or intersecting planes, or use lines to create the illusion of depth.

Use the images created to discuss the mood implied by the direction, placement, and/or thickness of line; or have students create a series of lines that suggest a mood or feeling. Have students complete all designs in black and white or in one color. You may wish to have students experiment with placing white lines on a black background, and black lines on a white background.

- Frame/Box

Have students create several designs using only the frame or box command. Encourage them to experiment by overlapping or isolating the rectangles, and to use several brushstrokes to see what interesting effects can be achieved.

Have students experiment by filling in some of the rectangles and leaving others open, or filling in areas where they overlap. Students can explore positive and negative space by further experimentation with backgrounds. For example, have students place white frames on a black background and then fill in the background with white. The outline form of the rectangle disappears, leaving a solid shape that may change the overall effect of the design.

Encourage students to save these designs periodically, adding to the design in steps or stages. If designs are saved in stages, the introduction of a shape that detracts from the overall design can be eliminated without losing the original design.

- Circle/Oval

Have students select the circle option and then create designs with only circles and/or ovals, a process similar to that explored in the frame/box assignment. Have students isolate the circles, overlap them, place one circle within another, and so on. Encourage students to enlarge the circle beyond the screen boundaries so that parts of it vanish, thereby creating interesting patterns of curves and arcs. Ask students to work first in black and white only, adding color after the design is finished. Remind them to save their designs in stages.

Jeremy Stratton
George Washington High School,
Danville, VA

Benjamin Carmichael
Clarisworks Paint
Tokeneke School, Darien, CT

• Positive and Negative Space

Once students have created several designs, have them experiment with the fill command. Ask students to explore a design created in a previous assignment by filling in the background and/or foreground. Discuss the effects of this process. Students might note, for instance, that shapes advance and recede, depending on the space they occupy and are surrounded by; filling in the background might affect the visual size of individual shapes or of the design.

Depending on how students make the fills, they might find that an entire composition is altered. Students can experiment further on their other designs. Students can load to the screen the saved original designs, creating multiple variations of the images. These activities will help students recognize the effects of positive and negative space on their

Other options may be available on the software packages you have. For example, some software allows the user to create a curved line or a French curve. You may want students to draw shapes by using the freehand sketch tool. The only limitation to using these options is the time that each student has on the computer.

The Elements and Principles of Design

Students may combine the elements of design on the computer in a variety of ways. They can also explore design principles, such as balance, repetition, unity, and movement. You might place individual elements on-screen temporarily, allowing students to study relationships before committing themselves to a final decision.

• Combining Lines and Shapes

Challenge students to create a series of designs on-screen that are a combination of frame, circle, and line. They might vary the size of the brushes used to create them, overlap and/or isolate elements, and experiment with black-and-white backgrounds.

Advise students to save designs in stages of development, allowing more freedom to experiment and providing both you and your students the opportunity to explore the process involved in arriving at a "finished" work.

Dana Mistretta
Fantasia, *Photoshop*
Randolph High School,
Morristown, NJ

Brandon D. Dawkins
Homewood-Flossmoor High School,
Flossmoor, IL

designs.

• Repeated Patterns

To create repeated patterns, students may use the window or cut/paste command. Have students design a small shape on-screen and use the cut command to capture it, and the paste command to reposition it on-screen. They might arrange the shapes in a formal, informal, or radial pattern. Some software will allow the user to flip and/or rotate, or stretch or shrink the image, adding to the alternatives available.

Although some software allows selection of a free-form shape of the picture, others require that the shape be defined within a rectangular shape. Advise students to define the shape they wish to save as closely as possible to the parameters. When that section of the screen is cut and captured, the entire rectangular area is defined. Therefore, the background of the shape is also defined within the borders of the cut area. Check with the software documentation for a detailed description of how the cut, capture, and paste commands work.

• Experiments in Color

If the designs created in previous activities were saved in black and white, students may load a favorite design to the screen for experimentation with color (or you may prefer to have them create a new design). If the design was saved in black and white, students may begin to explore a variety of color combinations, save them without losing the original, and reload the black-and-white design to continue the experiments.

Consider limiting students to one color option in their initial experiments. By selecting the fill command and the color of their choice, they may experiment with the placement of that one color in various parts of the design. Once satisfied with color placement, they can save the image with a different name, reload the original design on-screen, and select a different color to work with. Have students continue working in previously colored designs instead of calling back the original black-and-white drawing. They will likely achieve amazing variations.

Further explorations might include experimenting with various shades of the same color, or alternating the placement of solid and textured colors on foreground and background. Encourage students to explore several variations of color placement, saving each on disk. Although the colors available may not allow for traditional color studies, they do provide students with an opportunity to see the effects of color on an image.

The original black or white lines of a design can also be changed to a color by careful placement of the cursor over the line or lines to be changed. Warn students to be careful when attempting this: lines that intersect will also change color.

Have students create a slide show of the color experiments (see Displaying Images, below). Seeing the results of color selection and placement on the original designs as they unfold on-screen will help students note the changes in the overall effect of the original designs.

Note

Students' diskettes will quickly fill up with all these designs. Make sure you have several blank diskettes available for any overload.

Displaying Images

Have students combine their designs into a "slide show." If they have saved their designs in steps (saving each image after a limited number of changes were introduced to the screen), have them access those images so that the process of building the design is evident. When designs are arranged in this developmental sequence, you and your students will see the design emerge on-screen; the process of creating the design will be evident. You may stop designs at points of development to discuss why choices in size and placement were made. Students might enter into a discussion of how designs can be altered for a more pleasing effect, trying these experiments on-screen without fear of losing the original design.

An alternative is to have students create the same or similar designs and/or patterns with traditional media. Encourage students to compare and contrast the results, discussing the advantages and disadvantages of the different media.

Student Portfolios

Have students save their computer work on disks (preferably Zip disks since they have a larger storage capacity than floppies and can hold all of a student's work). If you have a scanner and the disk space, also have their traditional work scanned in and saved. More colleges are accepting student portfolios on disk each year. It is an economical platform for students, and, in some cases, more reliable than slides in terms of reproduction, shipping and handling, and showcasing the work.

Limits and Possibilities

The ideal artroom has a graphics tablet with every computer. However, even with the tablet and software programs like Dabbler and Painter, where the look and feel of drawing is quite natural, there is still a lack of precise coordination, and this can be very frustrating. Some students also find that the size and shape of the monitor is restrictive. These constraints pose boundaries for students who prefer finely rendered images or oversized work surfaces. However, some students will "shake" their quest for detail and pursue bolder renderings.

Because computers allow for risk taking and play, they may free students of the worry associated with experimenting and reworking ideas. Likely, both you and your students believe that many drawings, though they begin as wonderful ideas, often lose a quality of immediacy because of overwork and erasing. Students often complain that a drawing was better before the addition of color, and, indeed, many original drawings have been ruined through a mishandling of a medium.

With computers, risks can be taken because mistakes can be removed easily with the "undo" command, and original ideas can be retrieved if an experiment is unsuccessful. Students may thus feel freer to push a work to its aesthetic conclusion.

Students will not likely forsake pencil and paper for a graphics tablet and screen. However, as they gain control of computers, they may use them to plan works they will later transfer to a traditional medium, or they may appreciate the medium, with all its possibilities and limitations, and create works that exist only as computer images.

Allison Newman
Locked, *Photoshop*
Randolph High School, Morristown, NJ

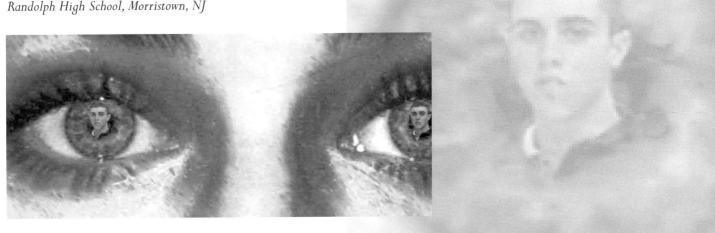

DRAWING WITH COMPUTERS

Drawing is personal. We begin to make marks on surfaces almost as soon as we are able to hold a pencil or crayon. While these marks are not made with the control most of us learn as we grow older and more practiced, they do give us our first forms of visual expression. The technical skills of the artist in rendering and illustration require years of hard work and practice at mastering those technical skills; they also require a trained eye and finely tuned powers of observation.

Many students are hesitant to take an art course because they feel they lack technical skills. They judge artists and their works (as well as their own talents) solely on the ability to render images realistically. If it looks like something, it must be art. Computers seem to provide students with an environment that promotes the development of artistic talent and creativity because students can play with ideas and imagery. Students who do not have technical drawing skills can use a draw program with menu commands such as frame, oval, and line to build their works or transpose images imported from other sources like photo CDs or scanners.

Brenna Moreland
Homewood-Flossmoor High School,
Flossmoor, IL

Strategies

To assist students in gaining mastery and control of the available input devices, and familiarity with the freehand-drawing option, have them copy a simple line drawing done for another assignment. A cartoon might work best. Remind them to keep the preliminary image simple; this is an exercise in control, and students will experience some frustration. Lines on the computer can appear jagged, and students may experience a "squirt" (a line that jumps across the screen for no apparent reason). Lines may not meet at given points on-screen.

Although students may use the zoom or magnify command for fine editing, allowing for more control and detail, working in the zoom mode is a slow process. Encourage students to try all the available input devices; they may prefer one device over another. You might also encourage them to use a draw program to build their images on geometric shapes, rather than working with only the freehand-drawing option. Students might also scan works done in other media, and work on altering that image on computer.

• Contour Drawing
Contour drawing teaches students not merely drawing skills, but also skills of observation. Follow the same procedures that you would with traditional media. Assign a number of different objects for study, or one object from several vantage points. You might notice that students using computers are less inclined to look at their drawing surface or screen than they might do with pen or pencil. Although the final image rarely resembles the object of study, interesting images often emerge. You might suggest to students that they overlap their drawings to create a composite work.

Students may wish to print out these images or try the assignment again in a traditional medium. Have them discuss the varying effects of these media and how the effect of the image is altered by the medium.

Siena Mair
Kitty, *Photoshop*
Randolph High School, Morristown, NJ

• Perspective

Have students select the line or box option to create a series of shapes that vary in thickness. Have them experiment with the different effects that can be achieved by placing these farther apart or closer together. By varying their width or placement, lines and shapes seem to recede in the distance or change direction. Encourage students to study how placement of an object in various planes on-screen can suggest distance. They can do this experimentation easily and quickly because the menu options place these lines and shapes with one or two simple movements; with the computer, you don't need a ruler to draw a straight line!

Suggest that students print a few of these preliminary drawings and use one as a basis for a drawing that they complete in a different medium. If students have several drawings with various vanishing points, you might have them create a collage or compose a picture with these varying perspectives, perhaps completing them in pen and ink.

• The Metamorphosis

An assignment that many art teachers enjoy is having students do a series of drawings in which an object "metamorphoses" into another, completely different object. Because drawing with computers is initially awkward, have students start with a relatively simple

object. After they have drawn the object, they can save the image on a disk or on the hard drive and can call the image back on-screen to work on directly to create the changes. Have students repeat this process with each subsequent drawing, saving each step of the process. Students can then create a slide show of their work. As each image "dissolves" into the next, an exciting emergence of each image occurs; students can actually see the transformation take place on-screen. If you have animation software, the drawing can be imported and come to life.

Using Menu Options

Several menu options can be used as a basis for drawing assignments, not unlike those discussed in the section on design. You might have students select varying brush options, or combinations of brushes with lines, frames, and so on. The menu options discussed can be used with contour studies or to explore perspective.

• *Brushes* Most software provides the user with several brushes that vary in length and width. Some are slanted at 45° angles; others resemble a dot or circle. Have students experiment with the variety of effects these brushes provide. Some software allows the user to define a brushstroke. The user may create an

Dana Mistretta
Inner Circle, *Photoshop*
Randolph High School, Morristown, NJ

irregular shape and "draw" with it as well. You may wish to return to contour drawings for students to experiment with brushstrokes or create new images.

• *Line* When students create contour drawings or studies in perspective, have them vary their brush so that they use broad or slanted lines, or lines that they double or triple. Discuss the effects that different line widths have on the image. Challenge students to experiment with the quality of line by selecting one of the available gray or textured tones. Students will discover that when they draw with these lines, the line is broken rather than solid, which creates yet another effect.

• *Spray* Have students use the spray command to create a picture in an Impressionist style. Ask them to build the density of the areas slowly and save their pictures at regular intervals. They can also use the spray command for shading and texture.

• *Magnify/Zoom* Although some may consider drawing pixel by pixel with the magnification tool a tedious process, many students will want to use this tool to perfect their drawings. You might also have students use the magnification tool to explore images imported with a digitizer, in order to study mixing for shades and highlights.

PAINTING-ON-SCREEN

When students first approach a canvas, their reaction is often one of awe. What can be put on canvas that is "worthy" of the medium? Of course, for some (adults mostly), the thought of blank monitor is as frightening as a blank canvas! Still, students are often afraid to begin a work—or afraid to continue once they have reached some success—because, so often, the wrong stroke of the brush, or the wrong selection of paint "ruins" what was a successful work. Computers may allay some of that fear, because they can be used to work out problems before they are transferred to canvas—problems of placement, color, or line.

Although the color limitations and limits of screen size still deter many artists from using computers, they can be an excellent tool for, at the very least, preliminary works or experimentation. Some students adapt more easily to these limitations than others. Just as there are artists who now claim the computer as their primary medium, you will find many of your students will create wonderful works of art with technology.

Christian Carmine
Homewood-Flossmoor High School,
Flossmoor, IL

Strategies

Advise students to keep their computer-created drawings simple and to create preliminary drawings in black and white. Many software packages do not allow the user to color over all colors, particularly colors with textures or that are part of patterns. Therefore, if students create an image in color, they may have only a limited opportunity to experiment with other color selections. However, if they save their drawings periodically, they may easily return to an earlier version if an idea is unsuccessful, continuing from that point, rather than starting with a blank screen again, or settling for an unwanted addition.

Once students become comfortable with the input devices, encourage them to paint directly on-screen. There are a variety of brushstrokes, tools, and color combinations from which to choose if you use Dabbler, Painter, or Painter Classic, and students may want to experiment with them. If a student is unsure whether an area should be blue or green, he or she can try both. If uncertain whether a sky would be more effective in gray, blue, or light blue, she can try them all. Encourage students to save each version and then return the original black and white to the screen in order to continue the experimentation.

Offer a variety of assignments: landscape and still life; a surreal use of color on traditional content; a

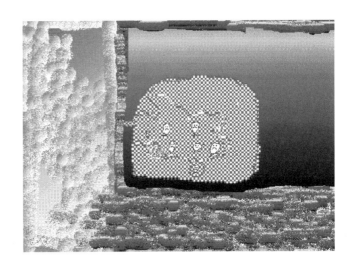

Jordan Rehlaender
Clarisworks Paint
Tokeneke School, Darien, CT

reinterpretation of an Impressionist or Post-Impressionist work, particularly the work of Seurat. Exciting images are sure to emerge. You may find that students who were locked into traditional modes of painting will break out toward Cubism, Expressionism, Abstract Expressionism, or perhaps a new style, completely their own.

Caution: be careful of disk overload!

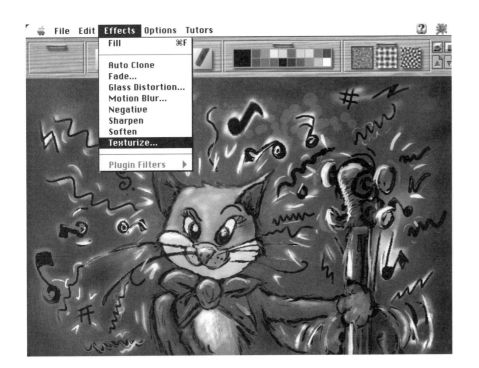

This sample screen from Dabbler 2 (more recently known as Art Dabbler) shows some of the powerful effects that are available in this relatively inexpensive program. Effects like Auto Clone, Glass Distortion, Motion Blur and Texturize used to be options available only on the most sophisticated software packages. You can also see that the tools or options are contained in "drawers" across the top of the screen. Dabbler screen courtesy of MetaCreations.

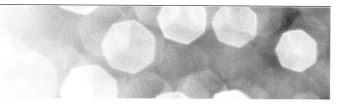

ADDITIONAL APPLICATIONS

The study of design and drawing and painting form the core of most K–12 art curricula. While applying design and drawing skills to problems and projects, students can explore a variety of media, so it's frustrating to find that no matter the medium or project, most students settle for the first idea that comes to mind. They're reluctant to push an idea, to explore alternative solutions. Further, once students put their first ideas to paper or canvas, they tend to stay with those images, even if they are unhappy with the results.

When students work with traditional media—paint, ink, metal, or clay—you may find that computers are helpful for preliminary problem solving. Students may experiment with ideas, images, and color; they may explore more options than they would with traditional media. Because students have little risk of losing or ruining images, using computers in the art curriculum for preliminary design work or as an alternative medium for design activities may provide them with additional opportunities to explore their artistic talents.

Layout and Graphic Design

Artists create layouts and preliminary designs for most of their works. Although layout is most often applied to plans for printing (such as for books, signs, or advertisements), planning is part of any art project.

Desktop publishing has become a familiar use for computers in industry and business, as well as in education. It merges text-editing software with layout capabilities, and combines this with laser printers for the in-house production of publications. The designer may juxtapose copy with graphics or photos, playing with the arrangement of these images quickly and easily. Copy fitting is also possible.

Although a system that includes, for example, a Macintosh, software (such as PageMaker), a scanner, and a laser printer can cost $4,000, prices are falling and some school districts see a system such as this as a good investment. While all districts cannot afford this, software programs are available that allow for some flexibility. Creating a layout is possible with some graphics programs such as Illustrator or even ClarisWorks by using text features and the frame or

Joel Hatstat
Billboard, *Photoshop*
Randolph High School, Morristown, NJ

Joel Hatstat
Community Phone, *Photoshop*
Randolph High School, Morristown, NJ

Siena Mair
Kids in the Bubble, *Photoshop*
Randolph High School, Morristown, NJ

box command. The placement of pictures and/or words is indicated by a frame or box and then positioned on-screen. Other frames can be added, deleted, and moved in the same fashion. The principle is that once a pleasing arrangement of these forms is reached, the actual text and/or images can be placed in their stead. Layouts can be easily created before actually working on paper.

A number of software packages (such as PrintShop, and The Children's Writing and Publishing Center) are dedicated to the design and layout of the printed page. You and your students can also create interesting layouts with the word processing module of integrated packages like ClarisWorks and Microsoft Word.

If your school publishes a yearbook, software may be available through the yearbook company. Many large yearbook companies have designed software that allows students to do layout, text editing, and copy fitting on the computer; layouts can be printed out for further work or editing, or left on disk. If the art department is not involved with the design of the yearbook, you may be able to borrow the layout software and explore it with students in various advertising and layout activities.

Photography

Computers have affected the world of photography in several ways: in the way we take pictures (with digital cameras and video cameras); in the way we store photographs (on disk); and by altering what we can to the photograph after it has been processed. Challenge students to take interesting pictures in almost unlimited numbers with a digital camera.

Most cameras store over thirty pictures; some, more than 100, depending on resolution. And, there is no processing involved. Students take the disk/camera to the computer to view the images. Many of the images in this book have been created using image-processing software like Photoshop, Color it!, and PhotoDeluxe. Applying computer-related technology to the world of photography is the wave of the present…and the future.

Architectural Drawing and Computer-Aided Design

At this writing, software for computer-aided design (CAD) is expensive and sophisticated. Many packages are in development and will be offered to schools at a price that is within the range of some school budgets. However, software is available to assist in the development of architectural design and/or mechanical drawing.

Art teachers have noted that this design and drawing software is being used in industrial-art departments in some schools. With this software, students can create shapes that they can rotate, enlarge, reduce, flip, or repeat. The first image—the design of a house, a room, or an object—is usually a two-dimensional line drawing. From the first drawing, the structure of the image can be built, cut away, and seen from outside or inside. Students can continue the process, add shapes, and manipulate the images.

This is a simplified description, but it gives you an idea of what can be done. Students can study architectural design and explore drawing techniques that use the geometric solid as the foundation of images.

Amanda Blake
High Mountain Road School, Franklin
Lakes, NJ

Animation

Computers offer a way to rapidly draw and redraw images; they create the effect of flip books without the tedium of repeatedly hand-drawing a figure. Students can use an animation program to create a frame-by-frame animation, or they can use a drawing program to create a figure, save it, and use that base figure to make alterations. When a series of images has been completed and saved, students can print out the various stages and create a traditional flip book.

There are several animation programs on the market that allow images to be drawn and sequenced to create the movement of the figure itself and the movement of a figure around the screen.

Animation is another area where computers can stimulate enthusiasm and excitement in your program. Programs include PROmotion Cinema 4D and, yes, even Kid Pix. Some animation can even be created with Dabbler. Animation is implied with programs like MetaCreations Goo and Gryphon software's Morph. Presentation packages (such as PowerPoint) can also deliver some sort of animation. **Note**: Be advised that animation projects take a considerable amount of time.

Dana Mistretta
City Life, *Photoshop*
Randolph High School, Morristown, NJ

Printmaking

Working out designs for linoleum prints or wood cuts on the computer provides students with opportunities to experiment with white and black backgrounds, and with the best balance of white and black areas or positive and negative space. Once they have achieved a clear visualization of a successful design, students may print out and transfer the design to the linoleum block.

Experiments in color for work in silkscreening projects can also be tested on the computer. Students might draw a facsimile of their work on-screen. After saving the preliminary drawing, they can experiment with different color combinations, trying background and foreground colors before making final color decisions. This allows for a more informed selection of inks and papers to use in silkscreened prints, linocuts, or aquatints. The same sort of experimentation can be done for textiles, batik, ceramics, and so forth.

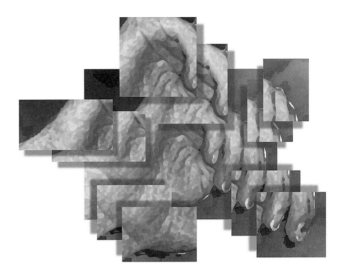

Michelle Hoffman
Photoshop
Randolph High School, Morristown, NJ

Set Design

There are few art teachers who have not been involved with the creation of sets for the school play or musical. You may wish to use the computer for preliminary drawings of sets so that students can experiment with them. A sophisticated CAD program can create the illusion of the stage, and thereby be useful for designing sets. Digitizers and scanners can also be used for this. Even if CAD software, a digitizer, and scanner are not available, drawings and experimentations in color and light can be tested on the computer before working on larger set dimensions.

Jewelry

Designs for works to be cast, cut, engraved, or molded can be worked or reworked on computer. If sophisticated software is available (such as the CAD software), students may be able draw their ideas on-screen, rotate them, and see them from different views. However, less sophisticated software also allows for experimentation in shape and design. Students can also design the enameling, engraving, and so forth.

Hope Dector
Prema II, *Photoshop*
Randolph High School, Morristown, NJ

Ceramics

On computer, students can work out the design of ceramic pieces, and plan their decoration. They can see their plans before beginning the actual work. If students experiment in creating their own clays and glazes, they might also use the computer as a database for information on successful formulas.

Textiles

The initial design and development of patterns to be done in weaving is a practical use of the computer. Some of the first art works done on computers were designs for textile patterns (see "Printmaking," above). Students can create textile designs with software that allows the user to work with a blank screen or to call a preliminary pattern to the screen and build on the existing design. A grid allows the user an exact area in which to work.

Because computers often imply color by laying colors next to one another, the illusion sometimes created in weaving can be accomplished on the screen. Students may save their works as "patterns" and use those patterns in the creation of larger images. They can also use the magnification tool to accomplish similar effects.

Consider having students use computers to create designs for various craft projects, such as needlepoint and embroidery. The gridlike patterning of the screen can be easily adapted to the design formations of these crafts. Two software packages designed for various needle and textile projects are PC Stitch from M&R Technologies and for young children Scraps and Stitches by Diane J. Hook from DJ Inkers.

Print Programs

Print Shop and similar utilities programs and CD-ROMs of graphics are in many school districts and/or homes. Simply put, these programs allow the user to create neat and legible signs, banners, stationery, or cards by drawing from a graphics library of fonts and shapes. These images can be quickly printed out on most printers. Students need not be able to draw to use a program like Print Shop. No input devices are necessary, and the software has been designed so that even young children can successfully create an image

with it. Students can use PrintShop without a full reading of the documentation.

With all these positives, what could be wrong? For one thing, everything done on these programs has a sameness to it. The library of shapes and fonts, while adequate for beginners, is limited. Users tend to rely on the images available, even if those images do not exactly accomplish the intent of the work.

The limitations of Print Shop have not stopped its use, and its very presence in schools should push you to use the software to its best advantage. Teach students how Print Shop and similar software programs can be used to create original works, and then lead them to see that there is a sameness to all that "canned" artwork, which can stifle creativity. You might use Print Shop, with a variety of font offerings, to aid instruction in lettering and in advertising.

Calligraphy is a craft not all art teachers have mastered, yet lettering and word placement is critical in discussing commercial design and advertising. Students can use Print Shop to select fonts and type styles that are suited to a message, or in the effective placement of words on a page. They might also make use of fonts in creative lettering exercises.

However, encourage students to take a critical look at what they create. We often assume that if something is visual, it must be art. Computers do not create art; artists do. And all the graphics libraries in the world will not insure a well-designed, well-executed sign. Assist students in using any clip-art software as an artistic tool.

Morgan Dillon
Cody, My Dog
Medina Elementary School, Bellevue, WA

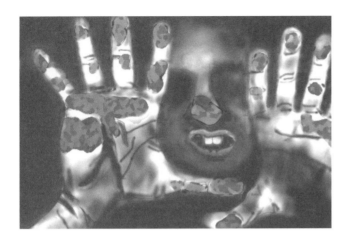

Tami Barrowes
Homewood-Flossmoor High School,
Flossmoor, IL

Graphics Libraries

Many of the popular programs on the market have a graphics library of images and fonts. Art educators may be accustomed to the term "clip art." Clip art is usually is in the public domain; it may be used for public or private use with little or no obligation to the original artist or designer. It is often used in advertising, on business cards, or in the yellow pages. Certainly, the availability of images has assisted classroom teachers in making lessons, worksheets, and tests more exciting. Some teachers encourage students to use these libraries in visualizing an idea for a story or poem.

In terms of an art program, how should teachers deal with these images? On the one hand, students who approach art with the attitude of "I can't" turn to these programs to create signs, cards, and banners. Their attitude changes to "I can." The use of graphics libraries hardly encourages originality, but they can be used creatively. Explore software that uses these libraries, and determine if and how it might be used within an art curriculum.

Because building on images is a valid procedure for creating, you might have students alter the original image. Have students study design principles repeating stored images to create patterns or to develop larger compositions. Using shapes from a graphics library might help students who lack technical drawing skills develop a sensitivity to design.

The use of graphics libraries has firmly planted itself as an acceptable practice in areas outside the artroom. Using these libraries for artistic purposes rather than fighting their presence is probably advantageous. They can be used well.

Jon Brower
High Mountain Road School, Franklin
Lakes, NJ

TEACH ART!

Five

The following are some profiles of teachers and their ideas for using computers and other technologies in their curriculum. There's no guarantee that a studio experience that is successful with one person will be successful for another, but the experiences of teachers profiled in this chapter should be helpful as you look for ideas, recommendations, and/or suggestions. The teachers who share their experiences here are excellent art teachers who have been using computers within their curriculum for some time.

Many of the activities that these teachers assign are rather traditional; they explore basic art concepts, artists, themes, and cultures. For instance, Bob Husth explores negative space with his students, and Susan Grossberg explores illustration. Many of the activities could be accomplished with traditional media. Both Bob Husth's and Susan Grossberg's students could have easily done the assignments in paints, paper, and/or markers.

Look beyond the suggested grade level for ideas you might use in your own classes. Although the molas activity, offered by Faye Scannell, is done with third graders, the activity could be adapted for almost any grade level studying various cultures. For example, a sixth-grade class studying Pacific Northwest Indians could create a pattern or design based on woven blankets or fearsome totem poles; a ninth-grade class might explore the basket weavings of the Hopi Indians. Adaptations are also possible with Anna Ursyn's project or with a broad theme like Susan Grossberg's illustration project. Finally, some activities are unique not so much in the concepts

explored as in the results that can be realized with technology. The results are different, not necessarily better. You may find a variety of applications of these activities to your own curriculum. The projects here are offered to give you a jump start.

Remember: You're the art teacher. *Teach art.*

Dustin Gage
This is the One
Arts High School, Minnesota Center for Arts Education, Golden Valley, MN

IN THE ELEMENTARY SCHOOL

Top: Anastasia Ivasenko
Bottom: Jordan Davis
Medina Elementary School, Bellevue, WA

Faye Scannell
Medina Elementary School, Bellevue, WA
Equipment: Macintosh computers, Hewlett Packard
DeskJet printer, 500 series
Software: Easy Color Paint

Faye Scannell has been using technology within the elementary art program for over six years, and has been using computers not only in her classroom during the school year, but also in summer camp. Her goal with computers has been to incorporate them within her curriculum as one more medium to explore.

Faye's students receive sixty minutes of art instruction every two weeks throughout the year. To make art activities more meaningful, she frames art concepts with broad themes and topics that students are studying.

Studio Idea: Molas of the Cuna
For this activity, Faye collaborated with a third-grade teacher, Carol Fielder, whose class has twenty-five students. In social studies, the third-graders compare and contrast communities of Washington State with communities in other areas of the world; in science, students study animals in their habitat. In art class, Faye combined those areas of study and introduced students to the Cuna of the San Blas Islands of eastern Panama, who produce a unique kind of needlework called molas. She showed students many examples of molas, a form of appliqué made by cutting designs through several layers of fabric, revealing patterns of contrasting colors. The oldest molas were typically made from three layers of black, red, and yellow, and were stylized images of animals, insects, sea life, and people. Designs are based on each artist's imagination, religion, legends, environment, and interests.

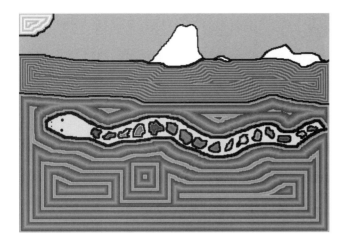

Nick Parker
Medina Elementary School, Bellevue, WA

During a discussion about different molas, students noted that designs were inspired by what the artist knew, imagined, and observed in everyday life. Rhythms made by the repetition of cut-fabric stripes, colorful stitches, and geometric shapes give the designs excitement and energy. Following the discussion, Faye asked students to draw the contour shape of a favorite animal on construction paper with oil pastels. They redrew the outline several times, using different colors to emphasize shape.

Later, in Carol Fielder's classroom, Faye briefly demonstrated a few of the drawing tools, as well as the color-gradient menus in MECC's Easy Color Paint. (These menus offer the selections found on most paint programs.) Students were then instructed to begin by drawing the animal that had been their subject of research in science class. Next, students explored the gradient menu options and filled both the animal and background space with colorful gradient patterns using the molas for inspiration.

This project continued in Carol's classroom over three to four weeks. Students rotated through the activity, using just two Macintosh computers.

Note
Students did this project with traditional media—construction paper and oil pastels—before doing it on computer. They did not scan in the images, which is an option, but drew them directly on computer.

Bob Husth
Warnsdorfer School, East Brunswick, NJ
Equipment: Macs and Windows PCs, Hewlett Packard printers
Software: Kid Pix, Flying Colors, Photoshop

Bob Husth has been using computers for several years. His classes average about twenty-six students. Grades 1, 2, and 3 have art once a week for one hour; grades 4 and 5 have art once a week for one hour and twenty-five minutes.

Bob's artroom has one Macintosh computer and one IBM. A Hewlett Packard DeskJet printer is connected to each of these computers. The students move between the computers easily.

Bob uses Kid Pix with first and second grades, Flying Colors with third and fourth grades, and Photoshop with the fifth grade. The program in East Brunswick fully integrates computers into the K–12 art curriculum, and Bob's school recently built a new lab with eighteen IBM computers running Windows 95. All have Internet access. Bob notes that students use the computer for about a quarter of their assignments.

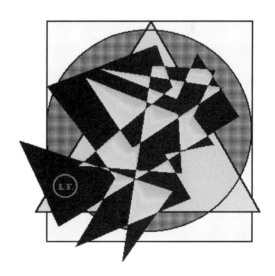

Lee Faber
Warnsdorfer School, East Brunswick, NJ

Eric Struening
Warnsdorfer School, East Brunswick, NJ

Studio Idea: Basic Design Concepts

Bob emphasizes basic design concepts. After introducing students to a basic design concept, Bob sends some of his students off to the computers in pairs. The remaining students work at their seat on the assignments, using traditional media. In a given class period, eight students can generate a work on computer. For many students, the computer work they create fulfills the assignment in part or in its entirety; other students continue to work with traditional media. Assignments featured here focus on negative space and radial symmetry, and Bob presents these concepts no differently than before he began using computers. The only difference is in the computer option to explore design.

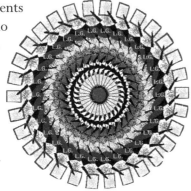

Lara Greenberg
Warnsdorfer School,
East Brunswick, NJ

Nancy Knutsen
Triangle School, Hillsborough, NJ
Equipment: Apple IIgs
Software: 816 Paint and Paintworks

Nancy uses Apple IIgs computers with 816 Paint and Paintworks, as well as MS Works for her word processing, spreadsheet, and database work.

Studio Idea: Letters as Design (using the computer to demonstrate a lesson)

Nancy used her computer to demonstrate how letters could be used to inspire design. On a large-screen monitor, Nancy showed students how to set up their paper into four sections, and then select four different styles of lettering for one letter of the alphabet (students had discussed styles of lettering in a previous class). The letter was to fill each quadrant of the

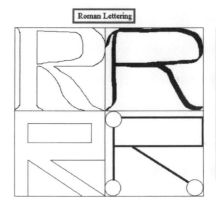

1. Draw four different styles of lettering for one letter of the alphabet.
   a. Roman Lettering
   b. The style you wrote the rules for.
   c. The style you drew the letter of which you read the rules for.
   d. Create your style of lettering.

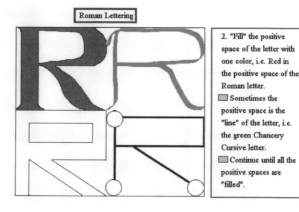

2. "Fill" the positive space of the letter with one color, i.e. Red in the positive space of the Roman letter.
   ☐ Sometimes the positive space is the "line" of the letter, i.e. the green Chancery Cursive letter.
   ☐ Continue until all the positive spaces are "filled".

paper. During the demonstration, Nancy experimented with several different letters and styles of letters. Next, she showed students how to fill the positive space of the letters with different colors. Students were able to see that the remaining white space was the negative space. Nancy then filled the negative spaces with a color different than that of the positive space. She encouraged students to try various patterns in their "filled" areas.

By using the computer, Nancy was able to demonstrate a variety of color fills and patterns, all done quickly and neatly. Students made suggestions, and she tried these as well. By saving this project on disk, Nancy could make changes in her presentation for future lessons, or give this demonstration to a student who was absent from class that day or needed to see the examples again.

Teacher-generated examples

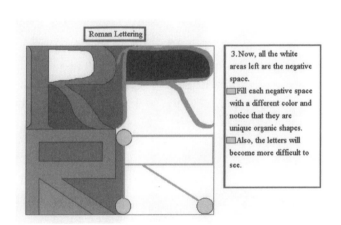

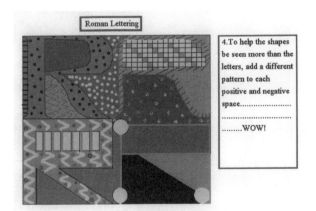

Kathy Vaughn
Hutchison Elementary School, Herndon, VA
Equipment: Macintosh
Software: ClarisWorks

Kathy Vaughn teaches elementary school, and, like so many of the art teachers who have contributed activities to this book, most of the work she does with her students is done with traditional media: paper, paint, crayon, clay, and so on. This activity offers an idea for teachers who have only one computer in their artroom.

Rachel Welk
Hutchinson Elementary School, Herndon, VA

Studio Idea: Miró (for the artroom with only one computer)

After a discussion of Miró and his work, Kathy hung a few Miró images in the back of the room, near the computer. She attached a written assignment to the images with an activity that students could do on rotation, two at a time, over the course of a marking period.

Kathy had her students begin with the spray-can tool in ClarisWorks. By moving the cursor quickly across the screen, students noticed that the background looked a bit like a painted burlap texture that looked like the textures in Miró's works. Next, using black and focusing on line and shape, students selected the pencil or brush to draw lines and shapes on the background. Next, using black, students selected a freehand-drawing tool or brush to draw shapes and lines on the background, making sure that some lines were thicker than others. Other colors were selected to add colorful shapes to the image. Students were asked to write a paragraph comparing their work with that of Miró.

Krystal McKay
Hutchinson Elementary School,
Herndon, VA

Jim Carrico
Wright Elementary School, Des Moines, IA

Equipment: Macintosh and digital camera
Software: PhotoDeluxe, Color it!, Dabbler, and Painter Classic

Jim Carrico is fortunate to be in a school that was selected as a pilot technology school about five years ago. In his artroom, Jim has one Power Mac, a printer, a color scanner, a drawing tablet, a laser-disc player, and a TV monitor. He has access to a digital camera. Jim's classes are forty-five minutes long. Students work with a partner on the computer. Before a student leaves the computer, he or she must complete an image and teach the lesson to the next student.

Studio Idea: Hey! It's Me! Self-portraits
Jim saves class time by taking a picture of each fifth-grade student with the digital camera. (Because a digital camera is easy to use, students could take their own pictures.) Jim downloads the pictures into a photo-imaging software package (such as PhotoDeluxe or Color it!) or into a paint program (such as Dabbler or Painter Classic). Using digital tracing paper or the cloning option, students have forty-five minutes to "trace" themselves and emphasize their features. They use various colors to fill in the selected areas.

Amy Morris
Wright Elementary School,
Des Moines, IA

Clint Robb
Wright Elementary School,
Des Moines, IA

This is an activity that art teachers can use again and again. If your school keeps portfolios of student work, have students view their self-portraits over the years. This viewing could be a wonderful learning activity for you and your students to study how their faces change as they grow up, and how their artwork changed as well.

Instead of a digital camera, you could use a scanner to scan in photographs of your students.

Debi West
Sugar Hill Elementary School, Cumming, GA
Equipment: none

What distinguishes Debi's project is that she has no computers in her artroom! Debi coordinated this project with the technology teacher and the first-grade classroom teacher, and produced a great example of how you can integrate technology into your curriculum even if you don't have a computer in your artroom!

Katie Kenline
Sugar Hill Elementary School,
Cumming, GA

Studio Idea: Native American Art

First-graders read Native American stories in class, and noted that animals were often characters in the stories. In art class, the students were asked to think of animals that they associated with Native Americans. After picking an animal (such as a horse or wolf), the students drew a contour-line sketch of the animal. They brainstormed for words to describe their animal. Later that week, during their technology class, the students used Kid Pix to illustrate their animal, reinforcing the contour-line sketch they did in art class. In Kid Pix, they added color to their animal and printed out their images. Later, students typed some of the words—using a variety of fonts and sizes—they had used to describe the animals.

With their printouts, the students returned to their art class, cut out their animal, and glued it to a brown paper bag or brown construction paper to give the impression of an animal hide. They also cut out their words and glued them on the brown paper. If time allowed, students added beads and feathers to their work.

Debi showed students images of Native American artist Jaune Quick-to-See Smith, and the students were excited to see that their own work resembled hers!

IN THE MIDDLE SCHOOL

Susan Grossberg
Franklin Avenue Middle School, Franklin Lakes, NJ

Equipment: 7 Macs; Hewlett Packard color printer
Software: Dabbler and ClarisWorks

Susan Grossberg has been using computers with her art students for almost ten years. In fact, her students' works appear in *Computers in the Artroom.* Susan has worked with the technology coordinator to make sure that, technologically, she is current in equipment and information.

Susan, computer coordinator Sally Lewicky, and coworker Gene Niglia have set up a wonderful computer segment of their art program. Susan has a computer/technology area of the room, where there are seven Macs, most of them Performa 5200s.

Class size ranges from eighteen to twenty-three students, and periods run forty-two minutes. Her program is divided into grade levels: the sixth grade meets every other day for one-third of the year; seventh and eighth grades meet daily for at least ten weeks (more if they choose an art elective). Students in each grade level use the computer for at least one project.

Susan has seamlessly incorporated technology into the art curriculum. What Susan's students have done here could be done in traditional media, but she and her students chose to use computers. With her students, Susan explores other activities that are accomplished only on computer, particularly those involving animation and HyperStudio.

Studio Idea: Under the Sea
This project, done by grades 7 and 8, explores composition and plans the layout of a picture. It began with a discussion of the need for a plan; in this case, a plan for what animals, plants, sea creatures, and so on, would appear at each *level* of the picture plane.

After brainstorming a list of what one might find under the sea, Susan demonstrated how to emphasize one level or the other by changing the size of the area assigned to each creature, plant, and so on. She also suggested eliminating a level altogether, allowing the student to focus on detail.

After choosing the layout of the picture plane, students began to research the items on the list. They went to the Web, used a CD-ROM, such as Encarta or another encyclopedia, or went to the school library

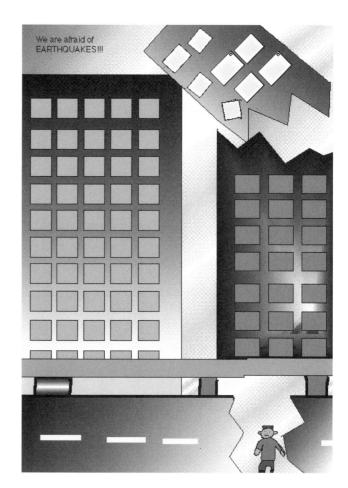

Jordan Adelson and Mark Bortz
Illustration: A Story Without Words
Franklin Avenue Middle School,
Franklin Lakes, NJ

Angela Chiang and Erica Bonanno
Studio Idea: Henri Rousseau
Franklin Avenue Middle School,
Franklin Lakes, NJ

and used books (yes, traditional resources can still be used!). After finishing their research, students completed their images. Most chose to complete their work on computer.

Studio Idea: Illustration—A Story Without Words (for grade 6)

To explore illustration, Susan and her sixth-grade students focused on the world of Maurice Sendak, specifically *Where the Wild Things Are*. Students discussed the relationship between illustrations and text: whether words are necessary to tell a story, and whether a good illustration can tell a story on its own. Students then chose childhood fears, a theme in the book, and set out on their own.

Studio Idea: Henri Rousseau (for grade 7)

This was an interdisciplinary project. After studying the work of Henri Rousseau, particularly his jungle pictures, students prepared to create their own jungle pictures. Encouraged to research plants and animals of the jungle, they explored the variety of species and the color and design of the plant and animal world of the jungle. This project, from the study of Rousseau to the printing of pictures, took twelve forty-two-minute classes.

Caitlyn Ginnity
Studio Idea: Henri Rousseau
Franklin Avenue Middle School,
Franklin Lakes, NJ

Barbara Delikaris
Florence M. Gaudineer Middle School,
Springfield, NJ
Equipment: One Macintosh LC580, Digital Imaging
Lab with 5 COMPAQ deskpro 4000 computers
Software: Painter Classic, Kai's Photo Soap,
Photoshop, Microsoft Office, PageMaker,
CorelDRAW, Art Dabbler, and Kid Pix.

Barbara has a Macintosh LC580 and color printer in
her classroom, but boasts of her "Digital Imaging
Lab." In a small, well-designed room, Barbara uses
five computers running Windows 95, digital cameras, hot lights, scanner, and color printer. Barbara
has been working with computers for more than five
years, successfully building her program.

Studio Idea: Photography—The Carnival

When the church next to Barbara's school started to
set up for a carnival, Barbara spotted an opportunity.
Armed with two digital cameras and traditional cameras, Barbara and her digital-imaging class of twelve
students walked across the school yard and into the
world of the carnival. The rides, the lights, and the
glitter all intrigued the students, and although they
had had the opportunity to discuss composition in

Jessica Gahm
Frozen in Stone
F. M. Gaudineer Middle School,
Springfield, NJ

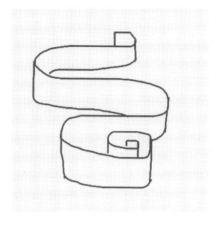

Teacher-generated example: Twister

class, here was a hands-on experience.

Teams of students took turns using digital and
traditional cameras during the shoot. Each student
shot several pictures, and they came back to class to
see their results. (Note: Seeing results right away is a
great advantage of using a digital camera.) Negatives
were processed and prints made; selected shots were
scanned and stored on student disks.

Students were able to critique their images in
class and by using Kai's Photo Soap (a photo-imaging
software package from MetaCreations) were able to
try out suggestions offered to improve their pictures.
Some zoomed into a section of a carnival ride or
booth; others cropped their photos to bring atten-
tion to the main subject; some decided to alter the
color of a section of the image. All of this was done
in two to four class periods.

Although the carnival provided excellent subject
matter, this activity could be done using a variety of
subjects, even your artroom. If your art curriculum
does not include photography and cost has been a
major deterrent, using the digital camera and computer to enhance and manipulate the image may give
you an opportunity for inclusion. (Note: Kid Pix,
Dabbler, and Painter Classic could also be used to
manipulate the photographs.)

Studio Idea: Twister—
Applied Drawing Strategies

When working with students to develop both drawing and basic computer skills, Barbara focused on the
spiral for this activity. Students used the mouse to
practice drawing a number of spirals on the computer

Yana Grishina
A Perfect Day for Walking a Dog
F. M. Gaudineer Middle School, Springfield, NJ

screen, saving their best effort to the hard drive or their personal disk. They learned how to give lines dimension and add opacity as they mastered this initial step. While a drawing tablet can make this project easier, students can use a mouse to manipulate and master a simple twister.

The second step was to incorporate the spiral or twist into one of the sketches in their sketchbook. (Note: Barbara emphasizes the importance of sketchbooks in her art curriculum). Everyone was amazed at the number of ways twisters or spirals could be used in composition.

Students then scanned their sketch into the computer and imported these images into a paint program. Final steps involved students in learning how to manipulate software tools to add foreground and background details and work with specialized color and gradient palettes.

IN THE HIGH SCHOOL

Nancy Norwood
Arts High School at the Minnesota Center for Arts Education, Golden Valley, MN
Equipment: 17 Power Mac 5500s, Nikon CoolScan, Negative Scanner, Apple flatbed scanner
Software: Photoshop 4.0

Nancy Norwood is a media arts teacher in an innovative, arts-centered public high school. Through the media arts program, students use elements and tools of current and emerging technologies to create works that express feelings and ideas. They are challenged to appreciate, analyze, and create works with film, photography, video, audio, computer arts, and interactive media. For their work, students have won over seventy regional and national awards, including the Scholastic Art Award. Their works have been exhibited in the *alt.media.youth* exhibition at the Museum of Contemporary Art in New York, and *Wired Youth* at the Exploratorium in California.

Each class meets approximately eight hours each week, and students are expected to work an additional five to ten hours each week in labs. Units include photography, computer design and animation, video, sound collage, film animation, portrait photography, and performance video.

Studio Idea: Color Digital Photomontage
For this activity, Nancy built on work done in black-and-white digital photography. With a class of sixteen students, she explored the history of photomontage.

Students discussed the work of photographers who used photomontage techniques and the various genres and styles that artists used to create photomontages. They also explored color theory.

Students preplanned each montage: they used color film to capture and save all images; scanned negatives and saved them; combined and layered three images from three different sources; and completed a prepared tutorial before beginning the actual photomontages. Further, since students were working with literary art students, they were expected to design each piece to accompany a piece written by a literary art student.

Thomas Page
Imagination From Within
Arts High School, Minnesota Center for
Arts Education, Golden Valley, MN

"I wanted to emphasize the creative
expression of our children. A child's
mind is so powerful that it is almost
like watching fireworks explode when
you see a child create and visualize…
The hand in the corner represents
society reaching out to our children.
The other image of a girl sleeping
represents society ignoring the
creative expression of children."
—*Thomas Page*

Amber Otto
Backyard
Arts High School, Minnesota Center for
Arts Education, Golden Valley, MN

"This image was created by composing
three separate scanned color negatives
together. Using Photoshop I slightly
manipulated the colors and designed
the image. The background is a green
field, trees, and a blue sky with
dramatic white clouds. In the field
I placed a red barn. Starting in the
foreground and going through and
out of the open barn door I placed
a gravel road. The bright, contrasting
colors make the image vivid
and intense."
—*Amber Otto*

Lorelei Jones
Homewood-Flossmoor High School,
Flossmoor, IL
Equipment: 10 Mac LCIIIs, 5 Power Macs 5200 (The tech lab offers electronic art, computer graphics, and desktop publishing, and has 31 Power Mac 5200s with Internet access.)
Software: Photoshop, Painter, Color it!, Studio 1, HyperStudio, PageMaker

Lorelei Jones has been working with computers in her high school curriculum for close to ten years, and has been very supportive of her fellow art teachers as they explored the use of computers in their curriculum. Lorelei is an integral part of TEMA (Teachers of Electronic Media in Art), a support organization that meets once a month to discuss and share ideas about teaching art with computers. TEMA also publishes a newsletter that offers helpful hints and keeps teachers aware of resources they might use.

Studio Idea: Collaborative Painting

When students start out on computer, they often do not explore the variety of tools that software programs offer. To break the ice and get them to paint on-screen with less hesitation, Lorelei has her students work on a collaborative piece.

During the first class, students created a 5" x 4" image area, and "painted" an object they had been assigned to bring to class. The students were asked to work quickly to complete the work in fifteen minutes. They saved the image (but kept the image on the screen), ejected their diskette, and took it with them as they walked around the room to see the works of the other students. Each student then added something to another student's image. After ten minutes, they saved the new image, ejected the diskette, walked around the room, and chose another image. This time, however, they were told to put the object in an environment or background. After another ten minutes, they saved and ejected the diskette, and selected a last image. This time, they were given ten to fifteen minutes to complete the image. They added to it or manipulated it to improve it, which usually takes two forty-minute periods.

After the works were finished, Lorelei and her students critiqued them on-screen. The discussion included tools and techniques used, composition, the emergence of style, and the concept of collaborative work, especially in the creation of multimedia and video and film projects.

Jacquelyn Sage
Homewood-Flossmoor High School,
Flossmoor, IL

Leroy Jones
Homewood-Flossmoor High School,
Flossmoor, IL

Christian Carmine
Homewood-Flossmoor High School,
Flossmoor, IL

Studio Idea: Surrealism

This project followed several projects that focused on cutting and pasting objects from and to alternative images; feathering edges; and rubber-stamping/cloning and blending with the smudge tool.

Lorelei selected the work of Dalí and Magritte for a discussion of Surrealism in the early 1900s. She encouraged students not only to look at the artists' works, but also to read articles about the works, to research the socio-economic climate of the time, and to read the works of some Surrealist writers and thinkers such as André Breton, Franz Kafka, and even Edgar Allan Poe. Noting that the Surrealists tried to create a new kind of reality, Lorelei mentioned their techniques: repetition, contradiction of size, juxtaposition of elements. Students were encouraged not to mimic the artists, but to try and create their own surrealistic work, their own "new reality."

After sketching out some ideas, students searched through their own photographs or through magazines and books to find imagery to use for their artwork. (Students could use a scanner or digital camera to import imagery into the computer.) After importing the images, students used a paint program to cut, paste, and manipulate the images. They critiqued their work, discussing not only the technical aspects, but also the kind of reality created.

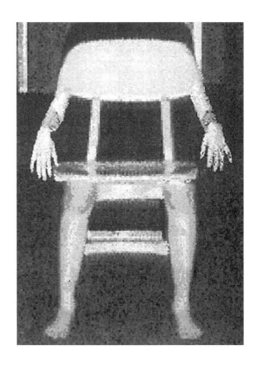

Lynn Schwab
Homewood-Flossmoor High School,
Flossmoor, IL

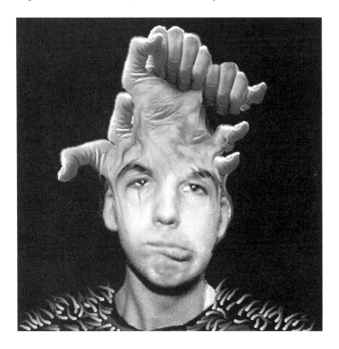

John Thoeming
Homewood-Flossmoor High School,
Flossmoor, IL

Shirley Cadmus
George Washington High School,
Danville, VA

Equipment: 13 Amiga computers, 2 Sony VATO computers (one hooked up to a VCR), an Epson 1520 color printer, 2 digital cameras
Software: Photoshop, Painter, PhotoDeluxe

Shirley Cadmus began using Amiga computers in her classroom in 1990. Today she has added two Sony VATO computers running Windows 95, a color printer that will print on just about anything, video equipment, and a good selection of software programs.

In Shirley's two-year, four-semester program, students work on still images in the first semester, moving images/animation in the second semester, and a variety of independent-study work in their second full year. Shirley's finest, award-winning artists come from this class. They have won many awards, including the Scholastic Art Award.

Studio Idea: Mixed-Media Collage

Working from previously created computer images, students chose one of their more successful printouts and glued it to a stiff board. They then expanded upon the image by using a variety of media: pencils, markers, pastels, and so on. Students could completely conceal the original image, or keep the original visible. They were asked to base their work on the works of artists previously studied, including Picasso, Braque, Bearden, and Magritte.

Shirley notes that this project is particularly successful with computer-art students who miss working with traditional media. Students could do part of the assignment on computer, and complete it in traditional media. It is also a good project for artrooms with only two or three computers that must be shared by all the students.

Elizabeth Gosney
Psychedelic Self
George Washington High School,
Danville, VA

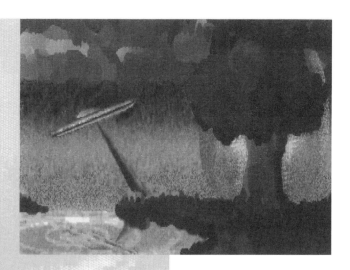

Megan Ward
Last Attack on Elmwood
George Washington High School,
Danville, VA

Studio Idea: Animation

Shirley Cadmus includes animation in her curriculum by dividing "animation production" into two phases: preplanning and production.

In the preplanning phase, students worked on a model sheet or storyboard that presented the animated characters, what they might look like from various positions, and what colors would be used. Students made flip books to explore how characters would move. Finally, they created a storyboard to indicate what the characters would do, the number of scenes, colors, how scenes would be composed, titles, credits, and transitions.

In the production phase, students first worked on black-and-white drawings to work out timing and movement. They then added color. Next, they created and added the background, repeating this process for each scene. Students animated the title, credits, and trailer; and joined all of the parts and recorded to VHS tape, adding sound and/or music.

Sound easy? It's not! And it is time-consuming! But students can learn a great deal, not only about animation, but also about the importance of preplanning.

Anna Ursyn
Department of Visual Arts, Computer Art
Graphics Laboratory, University of Northern
Colorado, Greeley, CO
Equipment: Computer Lab with Macintosh and
IBM computers
Software: Photoshop, Swivel 3-D, SuperPaint, Painter

Anna Ursyn spends much of her time in the computer art graphics laboratory, where she works with
K-12 art teachers, college students, and high school
students. Because she works in a lab, there is a computer for each student in her classes.

Studio Idea: A Journey to the Center of the Earth

This activity is related not only to Jules Verne's nine-
teenth-century novel, but more particularly to science and a geological exploration of the layers of the
earth. The activity began with an exploration of the
differing layers of the earth and their physical prop-
erties. Students saw several pictures of the geological
layers, including a sliced view of the earth and a cross
section of a human cell. They discussed the
macro/micro structures, noting many structural
resemblances in nature. Students also discussed
Verne's novel and/or the film adaptation, evaluating
the author's descriptions of human fossils, the bones
of ancient animals, and gigantic petrified vegetation.

Marianne Gatti
University of Northern Colorado
Greeley, CO

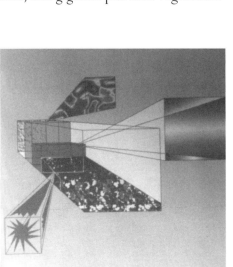

T. Alan Elrod
University of Northern Colorado
Greeley, CO

Emphasizing that they use their imagination,
Anna encouraged students to visualize all the structures and objects they would see if they boarded a
glass elevator to the earth's center. What would their
shape be? Their color? Their size? She then asked students to imagine a similar trip, this time to the center
of the human cell. What would those structures and
objects look like? Anna assured students that their
images could not be "wrong," because no one has
gone through such an experience. Students either
scanned in images and manipulated or combined
them, or they drew directly on-screen, using Painter,
Swivel 3-D, SuperPaint, or Photoshop.

CREATING A MULTIMEDIA
PRESENTATION WITH KID PIX

Getting Started

The hardest part is getting started, because, at first glance, this really sounds like a major project. If you take it apart one step at a time, you'll find that this is really quite manageable.

Working with Students

First, decide what it is you want to do.
- Do you even want to have students work on a presentation of some kind?
- What will the presentation be of?
- Will students work individually or in groups?
- Do you want them to use all original works, or can they scan in images from other resources?
- Will this include text? How much?
- Sound?
- Video?
- How much time do you want to allow for the project?
  Then you have to answer some technical questions.
- What kind of access do you have to computers and other equipment (scanners, digitizing cameras, and so on)?
- How much storage capability does your equipment have?
- How will this be viewed (on a small screen, large monitor, or by projection)?

Let's start simply and assume, for now, that what you want to do is have students create a slide show of their work. You want the slide show to include a brief student statement about the work, and you want the slide show to run by itself. Perhaps you'll use it at a back-to-school night or student arts fair.

Kid Pix Studio Deluxe® Courtesy of Broderbund Software.

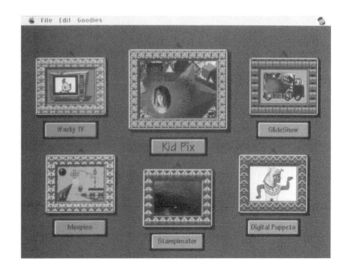

Kid Pix Studio Deluxe® Courtesy of Broderbund Software.

Then let's make some assumptions.

- You teach art education in an elementary school.
- You have one computer in your classroom (a Performa with 16 MG of RAM and a 1 GB hard drive).
- A lab is available to students.
- About half of your students have a computer at home.
- For this assignment, you are going to work with third-graders who have all had some experience with computers. There are twenty-five students in the class, and you meet with them twice a week. You divide the class into five groups.
Don't panic!

"Oh sure," you say. "What if I have thirty students in the class, and what if I meet them only once a week? And what if I don't have a Performa? What if I'm still working on an LC, or what if my hard drive is only 250 MG?"

Don't panic! One thing at a time. Let's work from here, and make some adjustments later.

You are going to use Kid Pix because it is a simple program to work with, and you know how to use it. It has some other points.

- It is available on all the school computers.
- Your students are familiar with it.
- It does what you want it to do.

Let's assume that you have already given your twenty-five third-graders an assignment for the computer that they have some time to complete. This activity is about combining the images into a presentation.

Begin by having students save at least one image that they created on the computer in a folder on the hard drive. You have labeled the folders "Group 1," "Group 2," and so on, for each of the five groups. Diskettes only hold 1.4 MG of information, and although you could easily save one student's image on a diskette, several students' work would not fit. If you have a Zip drive, keep a separate disk for each group.

Before we start creating a slide show, let's take a quick look at the Kid Pix slide show menu. If you haven't used this before, the screen you see has a series of twelve trucks, with a dog driving each truck.

Kid Pix Studio Deluxe® Courtesy of Broderbund Software.

(I know it sounds silly, but this really is quite a powerful program.) There are three icons on bottom of each truck:

- a slide (to import images to the slide show);
- a musical note (for adding sound; in this case, a brief narrative);
- a split-screen wavy-line thing with an arrow (for adding transitions). Note that although there are only twelve trucks on screen at a time, you can load as many as ninety-nine images.

Storyboard

Before starting with Kid Pix, have students create a storyboard. They determine the sequence of the slides—what will go first, second, third, and so on. They decide what will be said when each slide is shown (perhaps a brief introduction: "My name is Lenny da Vinci, and I created this drawing of my house. Then I added color to it. I also created this picture of a whale in the ocean.") Students also decide what transitions they will use from slide to slide, but that might come later.

Load Images

Once the storyboard is finished, students go to Slide Show, go to the first truck, and select the slide icon. When they find their folder, they select the image they want to be first, and—Hooray!—a thumbnail of the image selected appears on the side of the truck! Students continue this process until all the images have been selected. Students run the program to see if they like the sequence of images. If they want to change something, they simply move the trucks around by selecting a particular truck with the mouse, clicking and holding down the mouse button, and dragging the truck to the new spot.

Record Narrative/Sound

Then each student goes to his or her truck and selects the musical note. The student is brought to a screen that offers a number of prerecorded sounds. However, for this project, they will record their own words, so they select the microphone. Students record the script.

Select Transitions

Finally, students select the transition they want by picking from the sixteen available when they select the wavy-line thing. Transitions are important. Have students really consider what would be the best way of going from image to image.

Create Title Slides and Credits

Students may want to work together to create a title slide or two, and perhaps have credits at the end.

Hooray! Your third-graders are in fifth grade when they finally finish this, but what a good job they've done! *Don't panic!* That was a joke.

How long will this take? From the time students begin planning the storyboard to completion should take three or four forty-five-minute classes. That means that each group would need three or four class periods on the computer. Of course, the first group might take a bit longer, but those students can help the other groups.

And what if you don't have this kind of classroom situation and/or equipment? *Don't panic!* Let's say your program is different from the one described. Instead, you have more than twenty-five students, and you meet only once a week. And let's add that you have only one computer in your classroom—and it's an older Mac, an LCII. Moreover, you can never get any time in the computer lab, and you're not even sure that Kid Pix is there.

First, look at your curriculum. In your total K–6 curriculum, do you use computers? Is there a grade level where you introduce and/or use computers as a medium, or is the computer just "there" on your desk or in the corner if some student wants to use it? If you are not comfortable using computers or can't see how you might use them in your program, working with multimedia will be a monster for you. But let's assume you want to use computers and you want to have your students create some sort of multimedia presentation. Can you do it with just one computer and thirty students, meeting only once a week? Yes.

You have to draw upon your best classroom management skills here—but you do that all the time with limited budgets and equipment. When you teach your students how to use Kid Pix (or whatever other software program they will use), and you don't have a hard drive with a lot of space on it, have students save the images on diskettes that you have set aside with their name on them. After students have completed their computer assignment, demonstrate how to create a presentation. You might want to have each student create his or her own presentation, rather a group slide show. This will solve any problems with disk space. Also, if students work individually, putting together a presentation will take less time because you would assign each student just a few minutes of computer time.

By encouraging the students who go first to help the rest of the class, you should have this assignment done…by year's end! That long? Well, it could be. If you have only one computer and thirty students, it could take ten to fifteen classes to put all the students' work on disk. (For some of these considerations, see pages 51–53.) Evaluate your curriculum and the equipment available to decide how and what will work best for you.

An Alternative

Put together the slide show of student works yourself. This won't take nearly as long. Maybe students will be inspired to do something on their own!

Is It Worth It?

Ask yourself if you want to spend this kind of time on a project, and if it should be part of your curriculum. There seems never to be enough time in the school year to accomplish everything you want to do, and what you don't need is another project.

But multimedia is important. No, this project is not the most sophisticated your students could do; and, yes, it might be just a small grouping of some student images on disk, but through this project (or one like it), students learn to present their works (images created on computer and 2-D images scanned into the computer) in a unified, logical way. Further, to write a script for the presentation, students are required to analyze their work and talk about it—and that's a valuable lesson.

The point is that students can create a multimedia presentation with limited resources. They can use a simple, available program like Kid Pix to create any number of projects. Of course, Kid Pix is limited, and there are so many other software programs you can use. You may already have access to many of them. ClarisWorks allows users to create a slide

show; HyperCard gives an opportunity to create "stacks," or index cards of information, and also offers hypertext, the ability to create links to other cards of information.

HyperStudio is now the preferred software package in elementary and middle schools because of its ability to combine text, graphics, and video—and to create links to other "pages." Some high school level teachers also use HyperStudio, but students who attempt a large or complex project will outgrow HyperStudio and go on to Macromedia's Director. (However, Director is not as simple to use as Kid Pix. It's great at the high-school level, or for teacher use. But as of this writing, Director is too complex for elementary- or middle-school students, or anyone else without computer experience.)

With any of these programs, your students can create portfolios of their work; visual term papers; reports on just about any topic; or exploration of an artist, period in art history, theme, or style. Further, you and the classroom teacher or a subject-area teacher might work together to create an interdisciplinary approach to a topic or theme. Projects can range from science (endangered species, weather, molecular structures) to history (timelines, the Civil War, the civil rights movement) to mathematics (3-D modeling, fractals). The possibilities are vast…and exciting.

So, is it worth it? That depends on your goals and expectations of your students and your program.

David Joosten
Clarisworks Paint
Tokeneke School, Darien, CT

CREATIVE INPUT AND OUTPUT

A number of input devices besides the mouse and tablet are available, and the applications for a digitizer or scanner warrant a discussion.

You can capture an image with a digital camera and manipulate it on-screen using graphics software. Students might trace over images, explore their structure, or simply play with the color or composition on-screen. These images can be excellent teaching tools, particularly for students who think they lack technical skills. The digitized images offer an alternative means to be creative because there is no "direct" drawing involved. Further, because digital images are used in video production, your students will acquire skill at looking critically at video images.

By using a scanner, students can also transfer images (drawings, photographs, ads, and so on) to the computer screen. When scanning, don't stop with 2D images—try 3D objects as well. The effects can be intriguing and may give you some great ideas for further experimentation. Students can also get images from photo CDs or CD-ROMs and the World Wide Web, and use them much like scanned or digitized ones. (Beware of copyright law! See pages 105–108.)

Studio Ideas

Portraits

Have students capture the face of a classmate electronically and store that image on disk. If you have a digital camera, have students "sit" for their portrait; if using a scanner, you might use snapshots or yearbook pictures. Have students age the subject by adding lines and shadows; if this work is saved in stages of development, it might be possible to have that person grow older on screen through a series of images.

Have students change the emotion of the person in the portrait. Ask them to think about what changes when someone smiles or when someone is sad. Suggest to students that they turn the face or redirect the subject's gaze, alter the background, change the

hair and/or eye color, or even distort the face by stretching or pulling it in various directions. They might put the subject in a setting, or alter the subject's appearance to make it appropriate for an episode of *Star Trek!*

Landscapes, Still Lifes, and Performing Arts

Have students choose an image from a variety of photographs from a personal collection or from magazines. Once students have put the image on-screen, suggest that they change the colors of the captured image, insert objects, change the season, or alter the original to create suggested moods or feelings. Students might then study the image and/or use it as the basis for an original work.

Another assignment includes working with the director of the school play to plan sets, special effects, and lighting by using actual pictures of the stage areas. If your school or district produces a TV show, students might create exciting visual effects and graphics with the digitizer.

Output from Printers

If you have a printer, try a variety of papers. If you have an ink-jet printer and use photocopying paper, remember that the paper is not coated: the ink gets absorbed into the paper, causing the image to print lighter than expected, with a loss in vibrancy. There are several grades of ink-jet papers, the most expensive running about a dollar a sheet (you might want to consider it for a special group project). Several coated ink-jet papers run less than ten cents a sheet and produce good images.

Explore other papers as well. First make sure your printer can accept alternative papers. Most printers should be able to print on a flexible surface that is about the same weight as the paper you normally use. Have students try a variety of art papers with different bonds or textures.

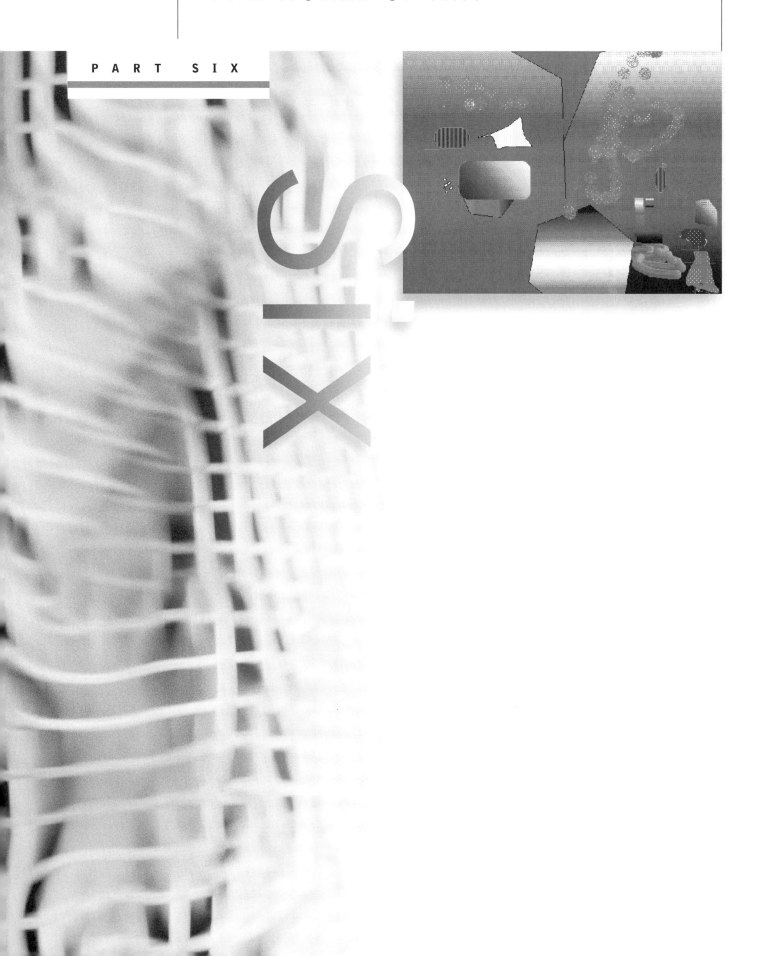

THE WORLD OF ART

SIX

A BRIEF HISTORY OF COMPUTER GRAPHICS

Twenty years ago, if you wanted to create graphic images on the computer, you had to program the computer: no software; no graphics tablet; just BASIC programming. The computer in most schools in the early 1980s was the Apple (no, that's not a misprint; before the Macintosh, there was "just" Apple).

The Apple IIe was a breakthrough computer that boasted 64K of memory, and graphic images were programmed with commands such as HLIN; VLIN; and Plot, Plot, Plot (sounds more like dance steps than BASIC commands!). When you look at the graphics in a games such as Myst, Riven, or the Carmen San Diego series, or in animation or computer animated movie such as *Toy Story, Antz,* or *A Bug's Life,* the special effects in movies such as *Jurassic Park, Independence Day,* and *Armageddon,* you can see how far we've come in such a short time. Computer graphics has quite a history, even though it began only in the late forties.

The Forties and Fifties

Can you guess the first users of computer graphics? The Department of Defense—followed closely by the aviation and automotive industries. Their use? The Department of Defense was visualizing trajectories for bombs. By the mid- to late fifties, scientists and engineers were using computers to visualize space launches, aerodynamic design, and flight simulation. In industry, computer-aided design (CAD) was used in both design and manufacturing.

Some of the early images from the complex programs were of visual interest. Although the mathematicians, scientists, and engineers who were problem solving with the computer were not artists, they approached many of the programs with a sense of the artistic. A mathematician once said to me: "A good mathematical problem produces a beautiful graphic image."

Does good math make good art? Does good art create beautiful mathematical problems? A great debate could follow, but let's push forward into the sixties, when artists finally got hold of computers.

Bit by Bit: The Sixties and the Emergence of the Art Image

The first computer images, limited to monochrome monitors and low resolution, were created with programs that addressed individual picture elements, or pixels. Because we have few records of works created on computers, presenting an accurate history of computers in the hands of artists is difficult.

For an output device, artists were limited to the plotter, and early images were often line drawings used as preliminary work to be transferred to other media like prints, paintings, or film. Still, we do know that the artists who worked with computers were working in industry or higher education. There were two reasons for this. First, before the development of input devices, artists had to work closely with programmers—or they became programmers themselves. Second, the cost of the highly technical computer workstations was prohibitive.

Engineers worked on developing tools that artists would later come to rely on. For example, in the early 1960s, Ivan Sutherland worked on a number of areas—including the sketch pad and interactive computing—that are only now coming to fruition. At Stanford in 1968, Doug Engelbart created the mouse for Xerox, but it wasn't until 1984 that Apple finally fully incorporated the mouse into its 1984 Macintosh computer. The rest, as they say, is history.

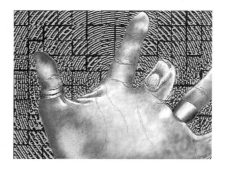

Steve Cyborski
Homewood-Flossmoor High School,
Flossmoor, IL

Caitlin Ginnity
High Mountain Road School,
Franklin Lakes, NJ

Getting back to the artists: work in industry and/or universities provided them with access to both expert programmers and state-of-the-art equipment. In the late sixties and early seventies, for instance, artists Lillian Schwartz and Ken Knowlton worked in Bell Laboratories in order to have access to the latest equipment. Charles Csuri, a painting instructor at Ohio State, traded in his brushes for a box of keypunched cards. These artists and others pioneered the field of computer art, working with programs and systems that today seem obsolete. Before the development of input devices, artists worked closely with (or became) programmers.

In 1968, a major exhibition of computer art took place. Cybernetic Serendipity was held at the Institute of Contemporary Arts in London. Since then, artworks created with computers have been exhibited at galleries and museums throughout the world.

In 1966, interested members of the Association for Computing Machinery (ACM) began a special-interest group, or SIG, for those members interested specifically in art and computer graphics. The result, SIGGRAPH, provides an organization for graphic artists, fine artists, and computer scientists to share ideas and insights. Each year, SIGGRAPH sponsors an art show at the annual conference. (For more on SIGGRAPH, see Part Eight, page 133.)

A Cumbersome Brush: The Seventies

By the mid-seventies, the reduction in the cost and size of computers led to personal computers; you could "build your own" for $395 with a kit from Heath/Zenith, and the Apple was being developed in a garage. Still, ten more years would pass before computers became common in schools and the home. Although many artists still use programming skills to manipulate their images, the development of input devices such as the light pen and graphics tablet, opened the field to other artists. For artists with no programming knowledge, the input devices allowed freedom of manipulation of images and a closer analogy to the artist's stroke. Although still cumbersome, these input devices gave some artists more access to the computer, and the computer became a potential tool for them.

Another phenomenon altogether really brought computers (and graphics) into the home: Pong. In 1972, Nolan Bushnell founded Atari and developed Pong as a coin-operated game, but its success led to the development of a home version. By the end of the seventies, we'd gone from Pong to Pac Man. Initially, the graphics were minimal at best. Those of you who remember Pong will remember the "blip" that moved across the screen. Space Invaders, Asteroids, and Pac Man (and Lady) followed, but these too were very primitive by today's Nintendo standards. For all practical purposes, the video-game industry died in the early eighties, only to be revived later, with Sega and Nintendo.

As for special effects (or FX) in movies, *Star Wars,* released in 1977, changed everything. The film set the foundation for things to come, with each subsequent film "FX-ing" the previous one. But more on that later.

Enter the Eighties

A surge of developments in input and output devices occurred during the eighties. Memory and speed increased from the 48K available on the original Apple to the gigabytes of memory available now. Color resolution improved—from four colors to palettes of millions of colors, and from screens of 280 x 190 (pixels) to screens that boast more than 1,600 x 1,200. Software was developed for creating drawings and graphics that were more interactive, and we can see results with little or no wait time for the picture to emerge, which had not been true for a programmed image. Also, input devices improved: the mouse and/or graphics tablet became essential.

As the interest in graphics increased, business and industry began to see that the visual would be critical to the presentation and understanding of complex figures and statistics. But most artists still shunned computers, looking at the machines as too technical, too costly, and too "cold."

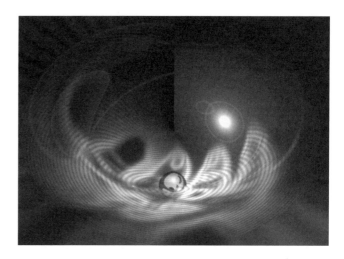

Matt Wright
Homewood-Flossmoor High School,
Flossmoor, IL

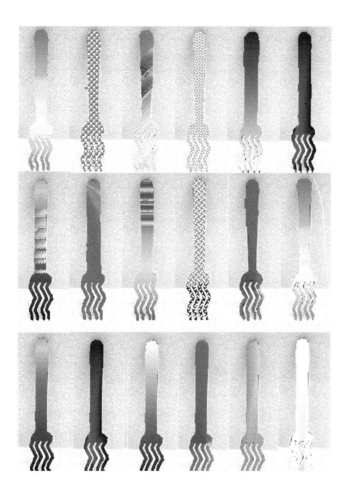

Apple Takes a Bite Out of Graphics

A leader in the field of personal computing, Apple surprised the business world with the success of a 48K desktop computer. As the average person grabbed hold of these first computers, all sorts of software—some of it with graphics—was developed. However, until the joystick and Koala Pad came along, graphics were the exclusive domain of programmers. Some interesting images were created, and not just by hackers.

As Apples entered school and home, users found that they could create some exciting images, with very little programming skill. Sample programs (long lists of computer instructions) appeared in many of the early computing magazines, such as *Creative Computing* and *BYTE,* and a variety of educational computing magazines. David Thornburg was (and is) a leader in that field.

Developments in computer graphics some time to filter down to the home market, but, by 1983, Apples expanded to 64K, and several alternative input devices were developed: the light pen, which

Eric Mayer
High Mountain Road School,
Franklin Lakes, NJ

Christopher Lopat
Clarisworks Paint
Tokeneke School, Darien, CT

allowed the user to "draw" directly on the monitor; the Koala Pad, a small graphics tablet that was a predecessor to today's graphics tablets but with much less control; and the joystick.

Sure, the Apples weren't perfect: there still were really only four colors available; resolution was poor; and the input devices were awkward. However, these developments placed graphics in the hands of anyone who wanted to use them.

Just as important was the development of software. Programs were created that were actually user friendly. The Koala Pad was packaged with Koala Painter. Blazing Paddles (from Baudville) was released for use with the Koala Pad, joystick, or mouse. But the software package that clearly put graphics in the hands of just about everyone was Print Shop. The ease of use and the number of graphic images available through the library discs made Print Shop the love of almost every computer user.

In 1984, the Macintosh was introduced, and nothing has been the same since! Although the Mac is the graphics machine par excellence, the Windows operating system did a good deal of catch-up work during the nineties, putting itself clearly in line for a place in schools and graphic studios. Moreover, many software packages (Like Photoshop, PageMaker, Painter, Dabbler, and even Kid Pix) are available for both Mac and Windows. Once the user is in the program, the programs look exactly the same. In time, there will be little difference between these two platforms.

The Nineties and Beyond

The 1990s brought several developments to computers and computer-related technologies. Yes, computers have become faster, bigger, more powerful, and cheaper (for what you get), but the real innovations lie with what computers are doing with—and to—other technologies. For example, multimedia has taken on a new role in education and training, and the Internet has opened an exciting window to information and communications: the World Wide Web. The full impact of the Web has yet to be realized, but take note: it's filled with wonderful possibilities.

Computers are also enabling the television industry—with digital and high-definition television—to make a dramatic impact on our viewing of the "tube." Cable and satellite technologies will bring us almost unlimited offerings. Computers and cable and satellite technologies will also impact the way we communicate with one another. Many "telephone companies" will carry more than phone calls, and these companies may not even be the providers of phone services!

Using the Web to communicate with family or friends (or to meet new people) opens up the ability to have visual contact with your "party." The cost is usually significantly less than that of a long-distance telephone call.

And this is just the tip of the proverbial iceberg. Things are changing more rapidly than a book could ever hope to describe, but *don't panic!* Once you understand the basics of how things work, the changes aren't quite so unfathomable.

A Digital Sleight of Hand: Special Effects

People are fascinated with special effects (often referred to as FX). The popularity of the blockbuster films of the 1990s like *Jurassic Park, Independence Day, Men in Black,* and *Armageddon* confirms that these special effects are an important part of the entertainment industry, not only in film but in television, games, music videos, and commercials.

Amazed by special effects, by all that appears to be, many teachers and students are asking me, "How did they do that?" It's not enough to be amazed by trickery; critical analysis of how these effects were achieved becomes a necessary part of aesthetic discussions.

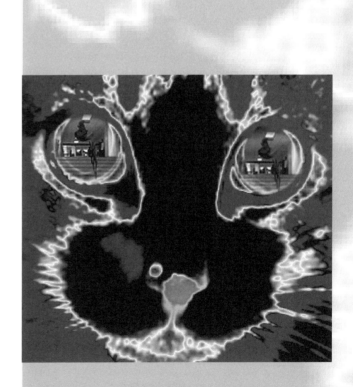

Early FX

Most of the special effects and transformations in the early days of the movie industry were done with make-up changes, mattes, stunt coordination, and a series of dissolves. Spencer Tracy changed before our eyes from Dr. Jekyll to Mr. Hyde; young and handsome Michael Landon turned into a teenage werewolf. Both of these transformations were done with make-up.

As the make-up artist "transformed" the stars, they were filmed in sequence; then a series of dissolves from sequence to sequence was used to capture the transition. If you look closely, you can detect the individual frames.

Morphing

Most recently I've been asked about morphing (or two-dimensional shape shifting). In *Terminator 2*, the T-1000 can change form. T-1000 can not only change form, turning into different people, but it can even morph from an inanimate object (like a floor or wall) into a person. The morphing technique is credited to Tom Brigham of the New York Institute of Technology (NYIT) and was first shown at SIGGRAPH in 1982. Interestingly, it wasn't until 1987 that Industrial Light and Magic (ILM) used this effect for Ron Howard's film *Willow*.

Morphing is short for metamorphosis, and specifies a 2-D process that manipulates a picture (usually a photograph). Morphing is done by stretching and altering parts of some real-world picture in a frame buffer (a frame buffer "holds" an image; each second of video represents 30 frames). In a sense, this is what Peter Sorensen in *Computer Graphics World* has called a "digital sleight of hand."

To morph T-1000, portrayed by Robert Patrick, ILM built a three-dimensional model in the database which they could call up on screen and examine from every angle. Once the image shape is defined mathematically, the computer can manipulate it. ILM technicians provided the computer with the first frame of the transformation and the final result; the computer mathematically figured out how to fill in the transitional frames so that the first figure mutates fluidly into the last. (This technique was first seen in *Willow*, where different animals transform into Raziel the witch.)

While morphing is very popular, it is just one tool in a wide range of digital manipulations. Another

Chris Majette
Misty and Cat 2, *Photoshop*
Randolph High School, Morristown, NJ

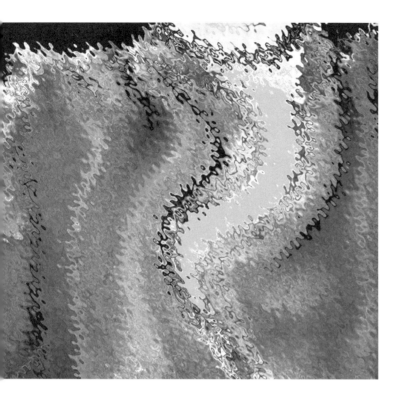

Allison Newman
Body, *Photoshop*
Randolph High School, Morristown, NJ

but because these techniques are within the reach of teachers and students. They need to know how things can be and are manipulated, so that they don't become manipulated themselves.

Is "Wow" Enough?

Despite all this new technology that elicits wows from people, we still must start with the artistic decision. How can I best use this technology for my purposes? How can technology assist the artists? Is the technology needed at all? Just because something is technologically possible doesn't mean we should do it; it certainly doesn't mean we have to do it.

In the 1980s and 1990s, special effects became a kind of movie star in its own right. However, although films like *Titanic* and *Saving Private Ryan* relied heavily on special effects, they were character driven and good stories. Let's hope that future films will return to good storytelling, and not just rely on special effects.

is the blending of stars from Hollywood's Golden Age like Fred Astaire and John Wayne into commercials.

The idea of enhancement is certainly not new. Models have been airbrushed for decades for magazines and product packaging. However, what is new is that with the enhancement and manipulation possible with computers, the model that appears on a magazine cover may not exist at all. The image we see is not a real person but a composite image: eyes fixed, hair altered, cheek bones raised, lips made fuller.

Computer manipulation means that the average viewer can no longer distinguish between real and unreal. We can't trust that what we see in films or videos are accurate versions of reality. Think of what Oliver Stone did in *JFK*. When Stone wanted to recreate history he shot with low-resolution film, making the scene look as if it had come from a hand-held 8-mm camera from the 1960s.

And so we are faced with an increasingly complex view of visual reality. And it's important to discuss, not only because we see this imagery every day

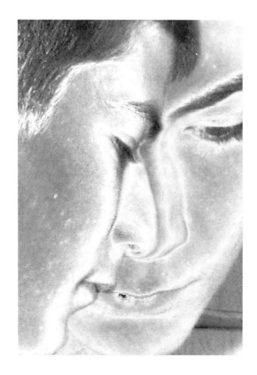

Hope Dector
Steve II, *Photoshop*
Randolph High School, Morristown, NJ

ISSUES OF INTEREST

Copyright Laws

Do you use Print Shop, Award Maker, or the other graphics software that comes complete with clip art? Do you and your students use a scanner? Do you download images from the Internet or use photos from CD-ROMs? While relying solely on graphics libraries and scanned images may discourage originality and creativity, it may encourage the visualization of an idea, a story, or a poem. You might use them as a basis for creating a graphics library, and your students may use them as part of an assignment—direct from their source or imported to a software program and then manipulated.

A caution: you may be in violation of copyright laws. Think before you clip.

Legal Questions

If you use images imported from other sources, are you "stealing"? Yes and no. How do current laws address the use of computer technology for image reproduction and enhancement?

- If artwork is provided within software, as it is pro-vided with Print Shop and Kid Pix, use of images is not stealing, but the use is limited.
- The images on photo CD-ROMs are usually royalty free, but what does that mean?
- When you "grab" an image with a video camera, you usually do so from life or video rather than a printed image, so the originality of the image is not in ques-tion. But when you use a scanner for photographs from magazines or books, are there limits?
- With a scanner or digitizer and a paint program, you can do just about anything to any image you want. But what are you scanning in, and when does the new image you've created by some sort of manipula-tion legally become yours?

A copyright refers to the intellectual and creative content of a piece of work when it is put in a format where it can be seen, perceived, read, and so on. The copyright law gives people such as artists, illustrators, photographers, and writers certain exclusive rights to control the original works they create for a limited time. This doesn't include ownership of the physical medium—only the intellectual or creative content.

You can't copy a protected work unless you have per-mission. Even when you buy a CD-ROM or videotape, you do not get ownership of the copyright. The copyright is held by the creator of the work, unless he or she has legally transferred it. You already know this about printed material, but it applies to artworks as well. You may use works that are in the public domain (publications of the federal government are in the public domain). A copyright for an image may have expired (copyrights can be extended and sometimes last for many decades), or an author/artist may have never protected a work in the first place.

Steve Cyborski
Flounder
Homewood-Flossmoor High School,
Flossmoor, IL

Many of us have made use of copyrighted works—but under the fair use principle. Fair use allows limited copying. The guidelines can be vague, but here are a few.

- If the work is copyrighted, don't use it. Famous cartoon/movie/TV characters are copyrighted, and it is difficult to get a license to reproduce these characters.

- The work should be for artistic or nonprofit educational purposes, but it cannot diminish the market value of that work. You take a major risk if you use scanned or digitized images anywhere outside the office or classroom without permission.

- Use of even a portion of a work may not be allowed. For example, you may want to use an image of a former movie star, or part of a painting from which you "extract" a subject from the background. Trouble! Even though a celebrity may be

thought of as in the public domain, or the painting may be in the public domain, the image is owned by a corporation, heir, gallery, or museum. Ownership rights may allow restriction to access. In some cases, though, the image has fallen into the public domain and can be used.

- Even if you do a great deal of manipulation of an image, there is still a question as to when that image finally (if ever) legally becomes yours. You can, for example, use a number of bits and pieces of images to create a new "whole." However, if the pieces you've borrowed are too similar to the original and if it damages the commercial value of someone else's work—trouble!

License Agreements

Have you ever read the licensing agreement that comes clearly printed on each software package you purchase? You know, the one that you agree to before you open the packaging that contains the diskettes or CD-ROM? Most of us haven't, but we should.

Clip-art packages and photo CD-ROMs may copyright either each individual image or picture (although this is rare) or the whole collection of images in a package. It is usually noted that you can use these images "royalty free." In other words, you need not pay a fee for the use of these photos and you are free to use any or all of these, as long as you do not make money from them. This means you can use such images for internal newsletters and magazines, but not for an advertisement or as a logo.

Obviously, there are other legal questions concerning the licensing agreement that comes with these packages, and the right to copy these libraries and "share" them with others. Graphics libraries are particularly tempting because they are easy to copy and/or transfer. Some are even available through electronic bulletin boards.

Corrie Bonham
Clarisworks Paint
Tokeneke School, Darien, CT

Copyright laws are complex, and lawsuits can be sticky. When there is even a small question, it is best to ask for permission to use an image. A fee (and that fee varies, depending on the image) is better than a lawsuit.

Here's an example of where you might cross the line. Several years ago, the senior class where I taught adopted E.T. as a "mascot" of sorts. As the yearbook advisor, I agreed that we should do a focus on E.T. When the yearbook pages were sent out, the printer immediately called to ask if I'd received permission to use E.T. I hadn't. Out came the pages. However, we could have taken a picture of someone wearing E.T.'s image on a T-shirt and run that. Go figure!

Kate Cassidy
The Project, *Photoshop*
Randolph High School, Morristown, NJ

The World Wide Web

Copyright restrictions apply to materials on the World Wide Web. This protects you, the artist, and writer, as well as others. You may not display copyrighted materials on your Web site without adhering to the restrictions requested by the copyright holder.

Dealing with copyrighted material is easy; but there are other legal issues regarding the Web that are still unclear, even to the federal courts at this writing. There are issues ranging from the rights to privacy, advertising and distribution on the Web, and even tax issues.

What is essential in discussing many of these issues with children is that there be an open forum for discussion on the ethical, moral, and legal issues associated, not only with the Web but with all new technologies.

Appropriation

When is appropriation appropriate? Electronic media has made imagery easily reproducible, which raises questions about the rights of artists and others who create original works, especially when they are exhibited on the Web. The following exchange in an Internet discussion group provides an illustrative example.

"In my opinion, art has no rules or boundaries, or at least shouldn't. So my work will take whatever source necessary to convey my message."

In response, someone wrote, *"If you take from my copyrighted work, I will sue you. Then we will see if art has no rules or boundaries."*

Does appropriation for personal expression or social commentary justify its use? Is it a violation of the creator's rights? Is the answer a matter of copyright laws? Ethics? Both? When, if at all, does appropriation become valid? Is appropriation acceptable when the original image has been physically altered or if the artist has changed its original meaning?

Another Related Discussion

An art student was ordered to remove Escher images on his Web site or face a lawsuit from the owners of the Escher site. Never assume that anything is in the public domain. Many homepages are probably in violation of copyright laws, so you would be wise to use only images that you or your students have created or have received specific permission to use.

Cameron McArdle
Blue, *Photoshop*
Randolph High School, Morristown, NJ

Piracy Issues: A License to Steal?

Many teachers believe that because they are teachers, they somehow have the right to just about anything, free of charge. We're talking specifically about software here.

Software is expensive. While site licenses certainly reduce the cost, buying multiple software packages is still costly. Moreover, some schools do not provide software for faculty members' home use. Add to that the difficulty confronted by poorer school districts that cannot afford software. The problems escalate at every turn.

Illegally copying software can be very tempting. Maybe you have a brother in the computer business, or you have a hacker friend who owns just about every piece of software ever created. The problem with making "just one copy" is threefold. First, it is illegal. Second, it takes money away from the manufacturer, thereby raising the cost to consumers. And third, it is unethical and sets a bad example to students. Many people are cavalier about taking software from family and friends and installing it on their computer, thinking that nobody gets hurt. But we all pay the price for this.

Censorship Issues

There is a great deal of discussion about children's access to the Web. Your school may even have installed software that limits student access. These control devices bar children from certain Web sites or types of Web sites. You should, however, also be aware of other sites that may contain images or information inappropriate to your students' age group or background.

For example, by encouraging young students to use the Web or a CD-ROM to explore museums and galleries, you may be exposing them to content or imagery that is unsuitable. You may not think your students are ready for some content.

All of us do a bit of editing when we discuss art images with students. We select certain slides or go to particular images in an art book. In a sense, we control what they see. *If,* however, we take students to a museum and let them explore, you never know where they will end up! The same is true with the Web or with CD-ROMs. When you invite students to explore, you give up some control. Just be aware that when you allow students to search through the Web or through a CD-ROM, you never know what will appear on their screen!

Cindy Moran
Flower Cubist, *Photoshop*
Randolph High School, Morristown, NJ

COMPUTER ART AND COMPUTER ARTISTS

The number of artists working with computers has grown, as has respect for works created by use of various technologies. As young artists emerge, they bring with them a seemingly natural ability to use technology in their work. Like most contemporary art that has yet to pass the test of time, the validity of computer-created work as an art form is still in question.

Artists create art, no matter the tool or medium used. But art created on computers has received harsh criticism from many critics. In articles from the 1980s, authors cautioned us not to be carried away by the dazzling techniques produced with computers. Artist Ken Knowlton, in an essay for *Computer Graphics* in 1988, noted that works created on computers were still in the "gee whiz" stage. These particular criticisms, more than a decade old, still hold true today. Work created with technology has been

Art Isom
Homewood-Flossmoor High School,
Flossmoor, IL

criticized as all glitz and glitter, more suited to film and TV than to serious art. The critics are hardly original in their comments. Criticism leveled at digital forms of art can be compared to that leveled at photography, another highly technical art form.

In the early days of photography, many critics disavowed the photograph as an art form. In *The History of Photography,* Beaumont Newhall described the divided opinions of the early critics who would, on the one hand, praise the art of photography in capturing truth and beauty and, on the other, denounce the limitations of the technology. Their arguments included the debate about whether photography was art or science, and discussions of the aesthetic value of photography. Some critics feared that photography would replace painting and remove the artist from personal involvement with the image.

You can see the similarities between the response to photography and the response to computer images. Today, professional photographers are enthusiastic about the new format. Richard Avedon and Barbara Kasten have joined digital artists Laurence Gartel and Barbara Nessim—as well as designers, cartoonists, and videographers—to explore the world of digital imaging.

Robert Tyson
Anything Is Within Reach
Homewood-Flossmoor High School,
Flossmoor, IL

ART, ARTIST, AND AESTHETICS

Melvin Prueitt was a pioneer in dealing with computer art as serious artwork. Certainly, others have followed, but in *Art and the Computer,* he presented computer-created works and discussed them in traditional artistic terminologies. And that's the key: work created with technology can be discussed in traditional artistic terminology. Many of the various traditional art styles and subject matter have been translated via computers and computer-related technologies by artists.

We can discuss works that have as their subject matter the traditional themes of landscape, still life, the human form, and abstraction—the same issues and topics discussed about more traditional art forms. Is a new jargon necessary? Yes, because the tools and the creative process involved in using those tools is different. Further, the artists themselves are different: many have grown up with this technology. Still, we can start from common ground, and that's essential.

In 1976, Ruth Leavitt, who edited the first book on computer art published in the United States, interviewed for her book several artists working with computers. She noted that the "type and quality of work produced on the computer depend on the artist who uses the machine and the program." As with any other medium, the type of work created very much reflects the style of the artist. Even in earlier computer works done by programming on cumbersome equipment, the style of the artist is evident.

The computer gives the artist new manipulative powers unavailable in traditional media, allowing him or her to repeat patterns, experiment with alternatives, and move and rearrange shapes and forms quickly and easily. More than this, the computer helps the artist perceive in a new way.

In an interview in 1986, Joan Truckenbrod, author of *Creative Computer Imaging* and whose work has been exhibited at the Museum of Modern Art, observed that a new art form will emerge; that images created with computers have characteristics that are different from other media. Further, when working in a studio, the computer artist works not only with one framework, but also with sound and sequence. Artists have begun to deal with simultaneity.

Truckenbrod observes that "when working with the computer, ideas intersect with each other in a multi-dimensional space—there's much more free association. The computer doesn't have the same linear step-by-step format as other media . . . When you think about the complexity of society today, this

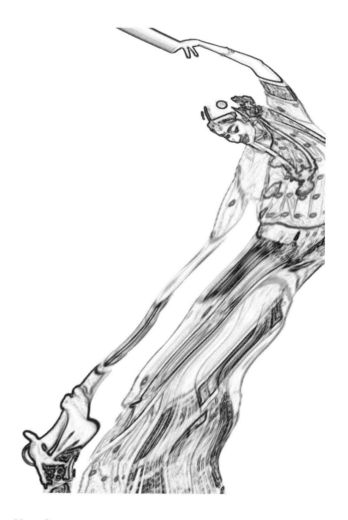

Hope Dector
Prema I, *Photoshop*
Randolph High School, Morristown, NJ

computer to explore some of the mysteries of art history, most notably, the *Last Supper* and the *Mona Lisa*. And Charles Csuri, a noted teacher and artist at Ohio State, has been involved in a number of award-winning animation projects done by his students.

Developments in technology—and, particularly, affordable hardware and user-friendly software—have brought some artists from their traditional place in the studio, working primarily on canvas and sketch pad, to an electronic studio, where the computer hardware and software become new tools. With technologies like computers, video, scanners, and digitizers, young artists and designers can visualize their ideas and experiment with them quickly and easily.

Electronic enhancement of images from other media is possible. New elements can be added to create composite images. Through these technologies, a new generation of art may have been born. Much of the technology is totally new to artists, and many are finding that they have moved out of the traditional studio and into the lab, TV facility, office, or home. Their work has come off the canvas and onto the video monitor.

Joel Hatstat
Collage, *Photoshop*
Randolph High School, Morristown, NJ

Katelyn Sci
Clarisworks Paint
Tokeneke School, Darien, CT

kind of art has a correlation to everyday life. It represents a new kind of problem-solving, a new kind of methodology." ("Computer graphics opens artistic options: an interview with Joan Truckenbrod" in *Computer Graphics Today,* August 1986.) While there has always been some kind of kinship between science and art (think of Leonardo da Vinci), perhaps the beginning of a new relationship between the disciplines is emerging.

Many artists, particularly those in the graphic arts, are using computers extensively—some as their primary medium, others as a preliminary sketch pad. The art that emerges is exciting. While some artists are still working in a more traditional fashion, others are exploring light, motion, and a merging of media.

If we look at a few of the artists mentioned earlier, we find that Ken Knowlton, an early pioneer, has continued to work as a computer artist as "developer/experimenter/inventor" and a "collaborator/teacher/writer." Lillian Schwartz has used the

Kate Cassidy
Self Portrait, *Photoshop*
Randolph High School, Morristown, NJ

Many people associate the use of computers with the graphic arts only, but this is inaccurate. Some artists coming to computers from other media (such as painting, sculpture, and film) have begun their work by treating the new media in traditional fashion.

Look at the work of fine artists who use the computer as their primary tool (perhaps beginning with Barbara Nessim, Char Davies, David Em, and Joan Truckenbrod), and discuss this artwork using traditional standards of evaluation. Some of these artists use a scanner or digitizer to import images into the computer, where they are manipulated fur-

ther; others use several different software packages or computers to arrive at their desired results. Their works range from traditional realism to explorations in 2-D and 3-D space.

Other artists are fashioning new forms altogether. For example, Harold Cohen has programmed a robotics system to produce paintings automatically, based on certain parameters. Stewart Dickson uses various computer technologies in evolving his mathematical sculptures.

Computers present the artist with the possibility of expanding artistic vision, of watching ideas grow, of playing with and integrating images. They also afford new possibilities for the artist—the added dimensions of time, space, and energy. These are new elements for visual artists to employ, but they present new arenas in which the artists can work.

Is it art? The answer is not an easy one, but Nam June Paik still has the best answer: "It depends on who does it. Art is what artists do."

Matthew Barter
Lighthouse, *Corel Photopaint*
Falmouth Middle School, Falmouth, ME

EMERGING ARTFORMS = EMERGING QUESTIONS

Ruth Leavitt notes in a recent article that "computer artists are reshaping aesthetic sensibilities . . . the two most prominent features of computer art are its interdisciplinary presentation and its interactivity... Essentially, computer art is a composition of ever-changing elements which depends on each participant's unique responses to create its final form. Although computer art is still emerging, it is time to recognize the control attributes—namely an interdisciplinary presentation and interactive viewer participation." (Leavitt, 1992; p.100)

While computer art should stand up to many of the measurements that more traditional works must stand up to (such as composition, technique, and content), new art forms also force new questions. Where does the artwork exist? How should it be displayed? How does time affect the artwork and our appreciation of it? What is the role of the viewer, and is "viewer" even the correct term?

Of course, there are other questions. We have to be open to the questions, not threatened by them. If we don't have all the answers, so be it; they will come in time. But simply because we may not know exactly how to discuss art created with technology doesn't mean we shouldn't discuss it at all. Even the ostrich doesn't really stick its head in the sand.

Marissa Ehrenkrantz
Frenzy, Photoshop
Randolph High School, Morristown, NJ

THE FUTURE AND SOME
FINAL THOUGHTS

seven

When I started to explore the use of computers in art education, almost twenty years ago, I was met with a good deal of skepticism. Many of my colleagues had no idea what I was talking about, and very little had been written about computers and art.

Art Education published a mini-issue about art and computers in 1983, and more articles followed in *Art Education, SchoolArts,* and *Arts and Activities.* Still, very little was written by art educators. Thankfully, that has changed. Now, articles that deal with technology and art and art education appear regularly in those magazines and others; and there are many Web sites, chat rooms, and mailing lists on the Internet.

But here's the thing: no matter how many resources we have available to us, we teach as we've been taught; and for the majority of us, computers weren't around when we were in school. Computers were in that "other" building, and there were those strange people with boxes of cards running around in there, always in a panic. No, computers were definitely not on my list of "things to learn."

Today, all that has changed. Computers are in our lives, in our homes, at work, and at school. Not only are computers part of our lives, they are also *essential* parts of our lives. And it is *essential* that students learn to use computers and computer applications. As teachers, we have an obligation to our students to prepare them for the future, *their* future. And like it or not, that future includes computers. What will that future look like? Some of the following might become reality.

THE ARTROOM OF THE FUTURE

So, what does the artroom of the future look like? Well, some things have changed.

- The traditional chalkboard doubles as a large, flat-screen monitor.
- Eight computer stations are in place in each artroom (all with scanners, video cameras, high-speed high-resolution printers), a library of art-related DVDs, and, of course, images that students have created as portfolios (electronic, certainly). Your Internet access is quick and reliable. Your classes' homepages are updated weekly by students, and you have an unlimited budget.
- All students carry small computers that have voice and handwriting recognition, and universal wireless access to the Web. There are no problems with speed of access or memory.
- Students are creating true multimedia presentations as easily as they write reports. These presentations include video, animation, sound, narration, and, yes, even text!
- Interactive video is part of every classroom. Students feel comfortable talking with teachers,

even in remote locations, so that distance learning and teaching are a reality, furthering the growth of the global village. With the smooth flow of video interaction, students have the

Ann Stammell
Buckminster Fuller
Falmouth Middle School, Falmouth, ME

opportunity for real exchanges of information. No matter where you are, or who you are, you can take advantage of the best—the best libraries, resources, and research equipment.

- Your artroom looks rather traditional, except for the computer stations. Students work on figure drawing and composition. Three students come up to you for help with the matting of the pastels they did last week. A group is working up a storyboard and accompanying DVD for the art show. Six students are working at the computer. They move seamlessly from traditional to not-so-traditional media.

- Computers are not the focus of this art program, but just another aspect of it, although an important one. Students sometimes use the computer to work out or nurture ideas. Some students use the computer to experiment with typography, color, and interaction of shapes and spaces. Others use the computer as the medium of choice (the emphasis here is on the word *choice*).

- Students use computers to explore images and information stored on DVD, visiting museums and galleries from around the world. Students use the Web for research and to interact with people of all ages and from all backgrounds; they view art in galleries they'd never visit in person, and talk with students from other parts

John Terison
Aliens, *Streamline and CorelDRAW*
Falmouth Middle School, Falmouth, ME

of the country (or world) who are working on projects like their own. On occasion, they have a chance to "chat" with an artist and discuss his or her work.

Too optimistic? To be honest, I do have nightmares. See the next page for some of them.

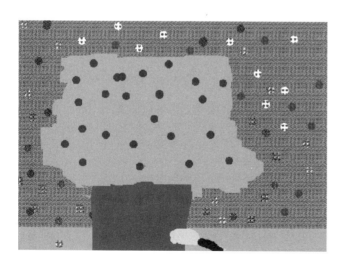

Melissa Madalon
Clarisworks Paint
Tokeneke School, Darien, CT

I SOMETIMES HAVE NIGHTMARES

There are times when I hear about schools that have received vast amounts of money and equipment before the teachers know what to do with computers in the classroom. My nightmares include the following:

- Schools receive technology grants for computer hardware and software, but no money is designated for training.

- Schools receive technology grants when what they really need is a roof, more classrooms, or more teachers.

- Schools are wired for Internet access without first establishing adequate electricity for the increased numbers of computers.

- Good teachers who feel very uncomfortable using computers are forced to use them in their classes. This often happens when training is not provided. Result? No one is happy; good teaching becomes strained at best; and good teachers get burned out. Not everyone has to use the computer for everything. (This, however, is not meant to excuse teachers from learning to use technology.)

- Because they can create images easily with computer technology, classroom teachers begin to think that they are actually teaching art. More jobs are lost for art teachers.

- Computers are shrines in the corner of the artroom— untouched and covered with dust and cobwebs.

- Artroom computers become archaic, as funds go to other departments.

- We're holding together the technology with glue and duct tape.

- Students are talking about digitized images and MPEG protocols while art teachers, brush in hand, paint Bob Ross happy little trees, unsure of what their students are doing.

Feel free to add your own nightmares.

Zach Rich
Star Wars
Falmouth Middle School, Falmouth, ME

BUT THE SWEET DREAMS of what happens

when everything is in place are also important to visualize. When it all works; when teachers have been trained; when students are in a safe and nurturing environment; when students have access to equipment; great things can happen. Students discover the wonder of learning.

Britta Briscoe
Jaguar Mola, *Easy Color Paint*
Medina Elementary School, Bellevue, WA

Chris Majette
Butterfly 5, *Photoshop*
Randolph High School,
Morristown, NJ

WHERE DO STUDENTS GO FROM HERE?

As art educators, we now have a body of work from which we can select images to discuss aesthetics; we have a history of computer use (though a short one) to use as a reference and for guidance. There is work to draw from and gain inspiration from. There is also the reassurance that today's computer artists have talent and creativity, not only in creating images on computer, but also in the more formal notions of what art is all about.

Teachers must ensure that students *know* that to be good at working on the computer is not enough. Mastery of Photoshop or Illustrator or Painter is not enough. What is essential is that which has always been essential: vision, composition, skill, and something to say.

Yes, art teachers should learn how computers can be used in the artroom to expand and enhance the education of their students, but that should not be to the exclusion of traditional media and art history and criticism and aesthetics.

When John Lassiter, director of *Toy Story,* was asked what software students should be learning in school, he pointed out that the software available today (such as Photoshop or Illustrator) isn't used in the movie industry.

What is important is that students learn the essentials of good art and good animation: writing, drawing, and character development.

Design is still design.

Drawing is still drawing.

Art is still art . . .

and a good art teacher is still

a good art teacher.

Don't panic! Teach art.

EFFECTS ON ART EDUCATION

New technologies offer bold and exciting promise for the future; they have the potential to bring new worlds and possibilities for learning to students, and new avenues for creation to artists. While technology not used wisely can diminish students' curiosity and creativity, the promise it holds for better education far outweighs the negative possibilities.

As teachers, we probably *will* make mistakes, but as art educators, our job is to reinforce the value of human creation and interaction—of the artist and the art image, and of our culture with other cultures. We must introduce students to media and methods of creating, the visualization and exploration of ideas.

Technology is a fact of life. I prefer to be optimistic. I am willing to predict that in another ten to fifteen years, computers will be incorporated into the art curriculum—for two reasons. First, our students today are using computers, if not at school, then at home or at the community library. College students who have no computer experience whatsoever are in the minority.

Second, what this in turn means is that graduating education majors have grown up with computers. They learned to use computers, and they will bring this learning to their classroom.

MY FINAL THOUGHTS

Recall Nam June Paik's remark, "Art is what artists do." Whether artists do art using traditional methods or new technologies, art remains art. It may be just that simple. Sure, there's a lot to learn, *and* we're fighting the obstacles brought about by budget crunches, by inaccessibility to technology, by lack of training. But the bottom line is this: technology is here, and it can be a wonderful addition to your art curriculum.

So, I encourage you to *use technology, teach technology, and teach with technology,* but above all else, *CREATE ART AND TEACH ART!*

Maxine Duckworth
Sunny Day
Falmouth Middle School, Falmouth, ME

BUYING INFORMATION

This reference guide contains several sections, all intended to provide you with technical information, and to offer additional resources to consult as you explore the use of computers in your art curriculum.

Hardware

Computers

Most computers are sold in bundles and include a CD-RW/DVD drive, modem, keyboard, a few software packages, and, sometimes, a monitor. If your school is making a large purchase of computers, you may not be able to make the final decision. However, the difference between Windows and Mac platforms is diminishing, and there may be no difference at all in five years. Just try to get the fastest computer with most memory and largest hard drive.

Monitors

Consider a wide screen or projection screen to facilitate classroom demonstrations. When you purchase a system, a monitor (and, if needed, a graphics card) is usually recommended, or the system is sold with a monitor. However, if you are in the market for a color monitor, look for a larger screen, such as 17" or 19". But note that these monitors are *huge* and may not fit in the space you've set aside for your equipment.

Printers

Printers that schools can afford have yet to attain the quality that art teachers desire. Be patient. Costs are coming down, and new developments in color printers have vastly improved printer output.

Black-and-white laser printers produce wonderfully clear text with near-typeset-quality print; they are often used in conjunction with desktop publishing systems. While expensive, these are decreasing in cost. New color laser printers are also coming down in cost and run in the $2,000–$5,000 range. The more expensive printers can handle large paper formats (11" x 17"), have a higher dpi, and run faster than the $2,000 printers. I recommend a Hewlett Packard ink-jet printer, a real workhorse. I have several Hewlett Packard 660s that are running for five or six hours a day, four or five days a week, and they just never break. Cartridges, though, can run up the budget, and you may want to get coated papers for students' final works. Basically, there are four types of printers (and a plotter).

Black and White Printers

Dot-Matrix

The dot-matrix printer forms characters by hitting the ribbon and then the paper hundreds of times per second with tiny pins. The printer uses continuous-feed paper and ribbons not unlike typewriter ribbons. It is probably the least expensive printer.

Laser

A laser printer operates much like a copier and allows reproduction of thousands of type fonts and sizes, as well as graphics. The image is electronically created on a light-sensitive drum, with a laser. Powdered toner sticks to where the light has touched the drum and is then transferred to the paper. Most offices have a black-and-white laser printer. (The color laser printer is becoming quite popular because its cost has come down.)

Color Printers

Ink-Jet

The ink-jet printer uses an ink cartridge that squirts small droplets of ink onto the paper. Of course, these droplets are almost microscopic. You can print on regular copier paper; the ink rarely smears; and the print heads don't clog. The quality of the images produced is quite good, especially on a coated paper.

Thermal Wax and Dye-Sublimation

A thermal printer creates wonderful images, but it is expensive, and sometimes slow. It offers higher resolution and richer color than an ink-jet printer. The thermal wax printer uses wax droplets of color that sit on the *surface* of the page. The dye-sublimation printers produce continuous tones and are perfect for photography. The output reflects the cost difference, but hardly enough to warrant the output of money by most school art programs.

Plotter

Fascinating to watch, most plotters are found in technical-drawing classes, because they work best with vector drawings. A plotter uses several colored pens to draw images point to point, line by line—a slow process, but perhaps an interesting option.

Input Devices

Keyboard

This has become such a standard to me that my editor had to remind me to include it! There are differences in keyboards, especially if you are looking at a laptop computer. Also note that there are special keyboards (such as large keyboards with large, colorful keys) for young children and for people with special needs.

Mouse

You must know what a mouse is! Joysticks and trackballs are also available, often used with games, although many artists prefer a trackball to a mouse.

Tablet

First, there was the Koala Pad, a small touch pad with about a 4" x 6" drawing surface. At a cost of about $99, this was a breakthrough in the early 1980s. In retrospect, it was awkward to use, and students had trouble controlling the cursor. Then there were those really expensive tablets. Tablets are now affordable and in a range of sizes. Basically, a tablet allows you to use a stylus (pen) to draw or paint on-screen. With a large work surface, working on a tablet corresponds more closely to intuitive drawing.

Although larger tablets are of higher quality, the little 4" x 6" pad may be your best buy, not only because of cost, but in terms of space. Where *would* you keep an 18" tablet?

Digitizer

If your school has a video camera, you might consider a digitizer. A digitizer lets you connect your computer to a video camera or special still camera and import video or still images to the computer screen. In other words, it captures and converts pictures to digital information and displays them on-screen. You can capture an image with the camera itself or from a VCR, camcorder, videodisc player, or DVD, and then send it to your computer screen. Once the image is on-screen, you can use various software programs to alter the image. Digitizers are available in still and video formats, in black and white or color.

Scanner

Like a digitizer, a scanner allows you to transfer images to the computer, but it is used mostly to transfer pictures or text to digital form. If you can afford only a camera or a scanner, buy the scanner: it's more versatile.

Scanners connect to your computer via a cable and/or some sort of interface that lets you capture, enhance, and transfer printed images. With adjustable hardware and software settings, you control the graphics size, resolution, brightness, and contrast. Typical editing tools include flip, rotation, resizing, and colorization functions. Images are usually imported to a compatible paint, draw, or desktop publishing program for further enhancement and printing.

Shakina Thomas
George Washington High School,
Danville, VA

The more expensive scanners provide better images but they require more computer memory and more printer memory. Be sure to research a scanner's memory requirements in order to determine if it is compatible with your computer system.

Slide Scanners

The scanners described above are for print (or flat) materials. They will not scan slides or film. Slide scanners are available as separate units or as attachments to flatbed scanners. The price for a slide scanner can range from $100 to $500.

Digital Camera

The digital camera is a popular input device, especially because quality has improved and the cost has dropped radically. Simply put, a digital camera works like a regular still camera, but with one big difference: images are not captured on film, but in the camera itself (a simple cable connection allows you to transfer the images to your hard drive) or on a diskette. The camera and diskette can hold anywhere from twenty to a hundred images, depending on the camera and the resolution at which you take the pictures.

Digital cameras—which range from the black-and-white QuickCam cameras for under $100 to color cameras with zoom lenses for $400 to $1,000—are great input devices for students. The great thing about these cameras is their ease of use. Make sure you get one with a good battery so that students can use the camera away from the computer or energy source.

Microphone

With sound capabilities built into most computers now, the microphone has become an easily accessible (and entertaining) input device. You can use it to record your voice, sounds, or music. Some computers have a microphone built into the system; others require an add-on microphone.

MIDI Devices (Musical Instrument Digital Interface)

MIDI devices allow you to create and play back music and other sounds. Using a synthesizer and sound clip libraries, you can add high-quality sounds to multimedia presentations.

Direct-to-Disc Photos

If you don't have a digital camera, you can take advantage of the new options for "developing" your traditional film, and they are as easy as taking a roll of film to your photo shop or pharmacy. Students can shoot a roll of film, drop the film off at a photo-finishing outlet, and receive a CD-ROM or a diskette of images, along with prints and negatives. The CD-ROM stores about 100 images, and the diskette, twenty to twenty-four images. Both are packaged with an indexed print of thumbnail versions of the images.

Professional photographers—as well as designers, musicians, cartoonists, and videographers—are enthusiastic about the new formats that allow them to explore the world of digital imaging. Uses in art programs (particularly where a photography department exists) are exciting. Once images are transferred to computer, they can be imported to favorite software with no loss of image quality. You can also buy photo CD-ROMs, which are usually theme-related: animals, space, travel, transportation, people, and so on.

Clip Art

You are probably familiar with clip art, the bane of many art teachers. Clip art first appeared in schools as part of Print Shop, a popular, easy-to-use piece of software. While most art teachers complain about clip art, there may be little we can do to stop students from using it. It's everywhere. However, it is possible to edit clip art (thereby customizing it), even in a program as basic as Kid Pix.

Generally, both clip art and photo images on commercially available photo CD-ROMs are royalty-free. However, check any advisories that come with the product.

Storage

There are several ways to store information for computer access. Your hard drive, a disk drive, removable storage (like a Zip drive) and CD-RW. When you buy your computer, it will come with a hard drive (measured in gigabytes from 10G to 80G), and a disk drive for the disks that hold 1.4M of memory. Many computers now come with a built-in Zip drive. Zip drives have removable storage and have fast access to the information on the disks. The disks themselves hold 100M–250M of memory (the equivalent of 71 1.4M disks). They are a great way to store large graphics files, presentations, and publications.

There are other drives as well, including Jaz drives (these hold 1GB and 2GB) and the newer SparQ drives (with a 1GB cartridge) from SyQuest. You can also buy external hard drives to store massive

CARE AND FEEDING OF COMPUTERS

Computers are not particularly temperamental, but there are some common-sense procedures in taking care of them.

- Follow all the instructions for starting up and shutting down your systems. While most systems are quite simple to operate, there may be a specific procedure to follow, particularly with computers that are networked. You or your students might print up a list of instructions to hang on a wall or distribute as a worksheet.

- As much as possible, keep dust, dirt, and liquids away from the computers. This is next to impossible in an artroom, but plaster, sawdust, clay, and the like have a way of finding their way into the computer. You might buy (or make) dust covers to throw over the computers when they are not in use. The rest of your hardware is also susceptible to dust and dirt, and you may want to make a cover for your whole system.

Disks

- Tell students that diskettes must be handled and stored with care.
- Keep the diskettes away from magnetic readers, such as the security systems in libraries.
- Store diskettes in a box or away from dust, direct sunlight, moisture, and extremes of heat and cold.
- Never insert or remove a diskette while the disk drive is running or accessing (reading or writing to) the diskette.
- Make backups of diskettes.
- Because the 3 1/2" diskettes are encased in plastic, they are quite durable, but they should be handled with care; they are *floppy* disks, not hard disks.

Note

No matter what the assignments or how you choose to use computers, remind students to save their work periodically. Not only will this allow you and your students to view the development of an image, but it will protect the loss of an image due to a power or system failure.

Caution

Beware of overloading your storage disks. Some software does not alert the user that the storage disk is full, and the image is not saved. While storage capacity varies—depending on program, disks, and computers—determine early on exactly what the disks you are using can store. Make backups of completed works.

A Word about Computer Costs

Part of the care and feeding of computers are the costs to operate them. Once you have a computer in your artroom, there are a number of costs—for paper, cartridges, and blank disks—that might not be obvious at first. Some school systems have a computer budget that handles all of the usual computer supplies; others do not. Find out early on if these supplies come out of your art budget. You should also determine who pays for computer repairs. If maintenance does not come out of a "computer fund," make sure you include maintenance in your budget.

David Becker
Platypus Mola
Medina Elementary School, Bellevue, WA

amounts of information, from 10GB to 100 GB. In an art program, these super-large drives might be used with video production and editing. Of course, the larger the storage capacity, the higher the cost.

More Than Storage, More Than Access

Some technology is not quite so easy to categorize. Technologies such as CD-ROMs and DVDs really go beyond mere storage, and the modem goes beyond mere access to the Internet. So, this seemed like a good spot to group them!

CD-ROM

Because of the storage capacity of CD-ROMs, books—even multivolumes—can be stored on them. The advantage? CD-ROMs eliminate the need for dozens of diskettes, are cheaper, and often come with an interactive training program.

CDs hold combinations of information, often as part of a multimedia system. Most of us are familiar with CDs that store music. CDs are called CD-ROMs when they store information other than music—such as books and whole encyclopedias. They are also used as storage media for large databases of information, such as those in libraries, including illustrative sound clips, documentary presentations, and games.

While some CD-ROMs are also designed to hold varieties of information like photographs (photo CD-ROMs), fonts, and clip art, the most exciting application is interactivity. With a CD-ROM computer connection, the *combination* of audio, graphics, text, and animation is possible. Not only can you "play" these discs, but you can also interact with them.

CD-RW

Simply put, a CD-RW is a CD-ROM on which you can save information. For example, if your students are working in video, or if you have a number of still images that students have put together into a presentation, you may want to put that work onto a CD; or you could create your own interactive CD-ROM (see above). A special recorder is needed to create the CD-R; the disk can be written to only once; CD-RW, allows the user to write on the CD-R more than once.

DVD (Digital Versatile Disc)

A DVD looks like a CD-ROM in size and surface, but it's much, much more. While a CD-ROM holds some video (although in QuickTime format), DVD offers

Yuriko Yamasaki
Clarisworks Paint
Tokeneke School, Darien, CT

huge storage capacity (from 4.7 to 17 GB), letting the user watch full-color, full-length movies on a full screen. While currently targeted to the home market (most titles are re-releases of blockbuster movies), the possibilities for education are exciting. With DVD, you can access data from multiple storage formats, take advantage of high-definition video (HDV), and use five-channel audio. That may be a bit confusing. Let's just say that DVD offers much better clarity, resolution, and sound than is possible with most computers today.

Video

Video is not new to artists: many combine video with installations or sculpture, and, in a sense, work in mixed or multimedia. Others explore video as it relates to performance art. The potential has expanded with new, affordable equipment and the use of computer technology to enhance and further manipulate the image. Work that once could be done only on expensive equipment in the studio—such as editing, animation, and titling—can now be done in the home or school. Digitizers allow video to be transferred to computer. Once that's done, students can do anything from simple editing to special effects. There are a number of programs available for a "standard" computer, but there is also higher-end equipment that a school or district might want to purchase, especially if the district sponsors a TV program shown to the community, or if students are pursuing their interest in video as an art form.

Modems
A modem modulates information so that your computer can "read" it. Text, graphics, and even animation and video can be sent from one computer to another. All you need is a modem, phone line, and some kind of communications software so that you can "talk" to your modem. Many modems come packaged with software, but you might already have communications software with another package (such as ClarisWorks). Or you may want to use an on-line service provider like AOL.

Most of the newer computers come with a built-in modem. As of this writing, the highest baud rate (or speed at which the information travels) available was 56K. (For more on Internet access, see page 42.)

With a modem, the potential of e-mail, the Internet, and the World Wide Web for education—and, specifically, art education—is boundless. Not only can you communicate with students, teachers, artists, gallery owners, and museum curators, but you can also view images and work together on-line to create an amazing collection of interactive learning experiences. (For more on this, see page 40.)

Software

You'll want to get a few software packages that are on *all* your machines, and a variety of software for specific purposes. These programs range from simple-to-use programs that rely on tools anyone can use and understand like a paint brush or scissors, to sophisticated programs offering complex drawing tools like matting and bezier curves.

Generally, more sophisticated programs emphasizing image processing, 3-D, or special effects would be found in high schools, not only because they tend to be more expensive, but because they require a great deal of time to learn. You might want to get a few of these packages for yourself so that you can prepare demonstrations for students; I have seen elementary teachers use sophisticated programs like Photoshop and Illustrator with their students. Let me add, however, that even basic programs like Kid Pix and Dabbler offer some of these tools in limited form.

Note: Any software packages listed here are suggestions only and are offered so you can get started. Try these out if you wish; better yet, talk to art teachers who are using computers and see what they are using. If you can, you might want to go to the Web and look for some ideas about software packages and art activities teachers have used successfully.

Software Packages
The following software is listed by recommended grades; suggested costs, the publisher, and computer hardware they will run on are included. Certainly this list is not exhaustive, but it may get you started.

The suggested levels of use were based on a variety of considerations, including ease of use, features, and documentation. Kid Pix is recommended for younger students, but that by no means suggests it cannot be used by high school students or adults (it is easy to use and may be sufficient as introductory software).

I have included sophisticated and costly software like Photoshop, PageMaker, and Adobe Illustrator because I have found them in use in several schools, not necessarily in classrooms, but in Administrative Offices, or for the school newspaper; even these more sophisticated packages could be used with younger students if you have sufficient time. For example, PageMaker, which is used by professionals

Kiernan McMahon
Ram Design, *Photoshop*
Randolph High School, Morristown, NJ

and is probably more than your art program needs, is user friendly and I have seen it used in schools.

It is difficult to give any accurate figures on cost because prices vary so greatly. For example, Adobe Illustrator (for the IBM and Macintosh) lists for $695; but it can be purchased through mail order catalogs for somewhere under $300. If you can, shop around for prices.

I have included the computers that these packages will run on. The magazines listed in Resources often have reviews of software; consult your computer coordinator or other teachers before buying software.

A complete listing of all the software available goes beyond the scope of this book; I have limited discussion to software I have used or that has been recommended to me by other teachers. If possible, work with software before you purchase it. Also, be aware that even software with very limited options may be of great use to you. Students often get so fascinated with all the options in more sophisticated packages that they never explore the software fully, and fail to create any images.

Features What input devices will the software accept? Does it have an undo command? A mirror command? How many colors are available? Can text be added to pictures? Is a graphics library available? Is a print dump included? Can the user cut and paste sections of images? Determine what features you need in your particular situation before selecting software. Keep in mind that students will be working under time constraints, so sophisticated programs may be unnecessary.

Documentation There are two points to consider regarding documentation, and they are almost contradictory. First, users often want to experiment with software before consulting the documentation. If the software requires extensive explanation before it can be used, it may not be practical, particularly when you're dealing with students and where computer access time is limited. Second, users must consult the documentation on occasion, perhaps to clarify how a command is used or why a command is not responding as the user thinks it should be. When this happens, the documentation must be intelligible and accessible. Consider how well the documentation is written and if it is organized so that the user can

Mark Tyburski
George Washington High School,
Danville, VA

find what he or she is looking for with ease. If the documentation is not well written, it will only confuse and frustrate both you and your students. The documentation should include a full description of the menu features and how to use them. An included tutorial can be quite helpful.

Because documentation is often *not* well written, you may want to include some money in your budget for reference books. Although several are listed in this guide, a computer store or large bookstores will also offer you titles that range from basic design to software-specific resources. These often come with well-written, clear, easy-to-follow tutorials.

Paint Programs

Paint programs allow you to create images directly on-screen by controlling the color and intensity of each pixel. In a sense, you are "painting" the screen. The pixel-based images are sometimes called raster images (because of the raster of lines that make up a television screen) or bitmapped images. These images are resolution-dependent; that is, the resolution, or clarity, of the image depends on the resolution of the monitor of the system in use. Paint programs allow you to freehand draw in a variety of brush shapes and sizes and in a vast array of colors.

Some popular paint programs are Paintbrush, Kid Pix, Dabbler, and Painter.

Elementary

Paintbrush	Windows	
Kid Pix	Windows, Mac	Broderbund

Elementary and Middle School

AppleWorks	Windows, Mac	Claris
Art Dabbler	Windows, Mac	MetaCreations
Painter Classic	Windows, Mac	MetaCreations

High School

Painter	Windows, Mac	MetaCreations
CorelPAINT	Windows, Mac	Corel
Photoshop	Windows, Mac	Adobe

Draw Programs

Draw programs are vector-based: they remember an image by keeping track of the end coordinates of each line. In other words, the image or object created is remembered as a series of mathematical computations or algorithms. The resulting images are of high resolution and precision. These draw programs are used in engineering and architecture (CAD programs) and in many graphic-arts applications, particularly in the design of packaging, logos, and displays.

Elementary and Middle School

AppleWorks	Windows, Mac	Claris

High School

Adobe Illustrator	Windows, Mac	
Adobe Freehand	Windows, Mac	Macromedia
CorelDRAW	Windows	Corel

3-D Modeling and Rendering

With 3-D drawing programs, you can create objects with $x, y,$ and z dimensions. As with draw programs, each object is made up of vectors, and 3-D modeling results in a wire-frame object that can be manipulated and moved through space. Rendering programs give these objects realistic surfaces, making them look solid.

Middle and High School

Infini-D	Windows, Mac	MetaCreations
Ray Dream 3D	Windows, Mac	MetaCreations
Bryce 3D	Windows, Mac	MetaCreations

Image-Editing Programs

Image processing allows the modification and manipulation of images and includes image enhancement (to improve the quality of the image) and image editing (to adjust the image, usually for use in a publication). The computer functions as a sort of electronic darkroom. With image-processing software, you can manipulate and alter an image that has been scanned or digitized into the computer.

Elementary and Middle School

PhotoDeluxe	Windows, Mac	Adobe
Color it!	Windows, Mac	MicroFrontier
Soap	Windows, Mac	MetaCreations
PhotoElements	Windows, Mac	Adobe

High School (sometimes elementary and middle schools)

Photoshop	Windows, Mac	Adobe
Painter	Windows, Mac	MetaCreations

Special Effects and Animation

Newer software allows the user to do everything from morphing an image or designing textures and backgrounds to the manipulating an entire image through digital video effects, including transitions. Most animation software is still based on cell animation, storing movements, and so on. Interesting effects can be achieved by using alternative packages that morph or allow the user to edit and manipulate video. Some programs, like HyperStudio and Goo, are not animation programs but do, in fact, allow animation in a nontraditional way.

Elementary and Middle School

Kid Pix	Windows, Mac	Broderbund
PROmotion	Mac	Motion Works

Middle and High School

Morph	Windows, Mac	Gryphon
Poser 3	Windows, Mac	MetaCreations
Ray Dream Studio	Windows, Mac	MetaCreations

Desktop Publishing Programs

A desktop publishing program allows you to set and manipulate text, create layouts, and import graphics. Several packages are available for use with all levels of students, from K to adult. These can be expensive, so evaluate what you will be doing with it in your school or classroom. Some yearbook companies provide these free to yearbook staffs. There are vast differences in costs. The higher the cost, the more you can do with the software. PageMaker and Quark are used by professionals to create newsletters, reports, magazines, books, and Web pages. Children's Writing and Publishing Center and Print Shop can only be used to do layouts. Also, remember to consider the time it takes to learn a program. Children's Writing and Publishing Center is simple to use; PageMaker takes many days to learn.

Elementary and Middle School

Children's Writing and Publishing	Windows, Mac	The Learning Company Ctr
Kid Works	Windows, Mac	Davidson
Print Shop	Windows, Mac	Broderbund

High School

PageMaker	Windows, Mac	Adobe
QuarkXPress	Windows, Mac	Extensis

Presentation Programs

These provide a framework for linking images or "slides" together, usually so that they can be viewed in sequence. Video, audio, movie clips, graphic images, and special effects can be incorporated to create a presentation or demonstration.

Elementary and Middle School

AppleWorks	Windows, Mac	Claris
Kid Pix	Windows, Mac	Broderbund
HyperStudio	Windows, Mac	Roger Wagner

High School

PowerPoint	Windows, Mac	Microsoft
Director	Windows, Mac	Macromedia

Word Processing Programs

Because you will use the computer for far more than artwork (lesson plans, recommendations, letters home, evaluations), you will need a word-processing package. Your school probably has one, and home computers usually come with some sort of word processing program installed. ClarisWorks, Microsoft Word, and Word Perfect are the most common.

Integrated Programs

Integrated programs combine, at the very least, database, spreadsheet, and word-processing modules into a single package. With these packages, you are able to move easily from application to application, and to integrate data from one module into another. Recent integrated programs have also included presentation, graphics, and communications modules. Microsoft Office and AppleWorks (formerly ClarisWorks) are commonly used.

Communications and Web-Related Software

Microsoft Office, AppleWorks, and Windows 95 and 98 all come with the communications software you need to access the Internet. Some packages also include a modem. You can subscribe to an on-line service or buy a package such as Internet in a Box or White Knight. For Web-page development, some of the new packages are PageMill from Adobe, FrontPage from Microsoft, and Claris Home Page.

Katrina L. Jordan
Clarisworks Paint
Tokeneke School, Darien, CT

Utilities Programs

There are hundreds of utility programs—such as virus protection, disk managers, and disk compression—that you might find useful in your artroom. These are usually not expensive, and many school districts have site licenses for their use, particularly for anti-virus programs.

Norton Utilities	disk repair	Windows, Mac	Symantec
SAM	virus protect	Windows, Mac	Symantec
Norton AntiVirus	virus protect	Windows, Mac	Symantec
Virus Scan	virus protect	Windows, Mac	McAfee
Uninstaller	disk management	Windows	Cyber Media
Spring Cleaning	disk management	Mac	Aladdin Systems
On Guard	security	Mac	Power On Software
FolderBolt	security	Windows, Mac	Citadel
First Aid	disk repair	Windows	Cyber Media
Conflict Catcher	disk management	Windows, Mac	Connectix
Stuffit	compression	Windows, Mac	Aladdin Systems

More about CDs and Videodiscs

After talking with people at several different companies, I have found that CD-ROM publishers change every fifteen days. What is perhaps more annoying is how fast these titles go out of print. Most of these are meant for a consumer market, and if they don't sell vast quantities in the first year or two, they're gone. Some are still "out there" but are difficult to find.

The same is true of videodiscs. Many of these are being phased out; in fact when I called two distributors they said they were only going to carry these while their current stock lasted.

So, instead of trying to create a list of all the software and publishers, I have listed only those that have been around for awhile, like *With Open Eyes.*

And, since teachers deal mainly with large resellers instead of publishers, I list them too.

Resellers/Suppliers:
Educational Resources: 1-800-624-2926
Educorp: 1-800-843-9497
Scholastic: 1-800-724-4811
Forest Technologies: 1-800-544-3356
Sax Arts & Crafts: 1-800-558-6696

Resellers or suppliers offer a wide variety of products and have catalogs available for product and pricing information.

RESOURCES

The following resources may be of assistance as you set out to establish a network of additional guides and resource materials for you and your students to use. I have included traditional and new resources as well as some non-traditional resources you might want to consider.

Traditional Resources

Books

When I wrote *Computers in the Artroom* fifteen years ago, I was lucky if I found more than a few books on computers in any bookstore. Now in any of the major bookstores, there are not just shelves of computer-related books but aisles of them.

In general, several types of computer books are helpful: software-specific books (e.g., on Photoshop, Illustrator, PowerPoint, or Painter), computer graphics or design books, books on multimedia and the Internet or Web, and books geared to teachers. There are several publishers whose books I am generally pleased with: Hayden Books, IDG-Ziff-Davis, and Peachpit Press. Certainly there are other publishers, but this is a start.

The following books contain a wide variety of computer images and may offer you and your students ideas and inspiration. My advice is to go to a bookstore or to a Web site like amazon.com and look for information in your area of concern or interest. One of my favorite series of books is the *Dummies* series now published by Wiley (www.wiley.com, www.dummies.com, and www.idg.com). These books are fun and a bit irreverent, and they assume you know next to nothing. You can skip around and find just what it is you need to know, or start at the beginning and go straight through. Some of their titles are *Macs for Teachers, The Internet for Teachers, Multimedia and CD-ROM for Dummies, The Internet for Dummies,* and *Photoshop for Dummies.*

Titles from Peachpit Press (www.peachpit.com) also has a lot of interesting titles, including *Designing Multimedia* by Lisa Lopuck, *Non-Designers Web Book* by Robin Williams, and *Non-Designers Design Book* by Robin Williams.

Teacher Created Materials offers *Managing Technology in the Classroom (Grades K–6), Managing Technology in the Middle School Classroom,* and *Integrating Technology in the Curriculum.* Their series on Technology Tools for Terrified Teachers includes *Kid Pix for Terrified Teachers* and *HyperStudio for Terrified Teachers.*

Other books include (but are not limited to):

Ashford, Janet (2001). *The Arts and Crafts Computer: Using Your Computer as an Artist's Tool.* Peachpit Press.

Baird, McDonald, Pittman and Turnbull (1993). *The Graphics of Communication: Methods, Media and Technology.* 6th ed. Harcourt Brace.

Bourgess, Jean (1997). *Color Bytes: Blending the Art and Science of Color.* Davis Publications, Inc.

Clark, David (1995). *Internet Essentials.* 2nd ed. Que College Press.

Em, David (1988). *The Art of David Em* Harry Abrams, Inc.

Fahey, M. (1995). *Web Publishers Design Guide for Macintosh.* Coriales Group Books.

Goodman, Cynthia (1987). *Digital Visions: Computers and Art.* Harry Abrams, Inc.

Holtzman, Steven (1997). *Digital Mosaics: The Aesthetics of Cyberspace.* Peachpit Press.

Jacobson, Linda, ed. (1992). *Cyberarts: Exploring Art and Technology.* Peachpit Press.

Kerlow, Isaac (1997). *Art of 3-D Computer Animation.* Van Nostrand Reinhart.

Kerlow, Isaac (2000). *The Art of 3-D Computer Animation and Imaging.* Wiley and Sons.

Leavitt, Ruth (1976). *Artist and Computer.* Hastings House.

Pickover, Clifford (1992). *Computers and the Imagination.* St. Martin's Press.

Prueitt, Melvin (1984). *Art and the Computer.*
    McGraw Hill.
Weinman, L. (1996). *Designing Web Pages.* New
    Riders Press.
Williams, Robin and Tollette, John (2000). *Robin
    Williams Design Workshop.* Peachpit Press.

Magazines
There are numerous magazines to consult. I selected
the following titles because I have used them and find
them not too technical; and they are relatively easy to
get hold of. All are available in college or university
libraries; some may be in your school library. The
more popular ones are available at any good news-
stand. Many of these magazines have Web sites.

Art Education
You may already be familiar with the following mag-
azines for art educators. Computer-related articles
sometimes appear in them.
Arts and Activities (www.artsandactivities.com)
*Art Education: The Journal of the National Art Education
Association* (www.naea-reston.org)
Studies in Art Education (www.naea-reston.org)
SchoolArts (www.davis-art.com)

Computer Graphics
The following magazines can be quite technical at
times. However, they contain information about
state-of-the-art technologies, and they usually have
great photos.
CD-ROM OnLine (www.nsi.web.com)
Computer Arts (www.computerarts.co.uk)
Computer Graphics World (cgw.pennnet.com/home.cfm)
Computer Graphics (www.siggraph.org)
Leonardo (mitpress.mit.edu/e-journals/Leonardo)
MediaNews (www.medianews.com)

Educational Computing
Each of these magazines, while not art-specific, has
overviews of computers in education, new products,
software reviews, and, often, art-related topics.
These may be available in your school library.
Creative Classroom (www.creativeclassroom.org)
Electronic School (www.electronic-school.com)
Online Educator (www.ole.net/ole)
Syllabus (www.syllabus.com)
T.H.E. Journal (www.thejournal.com)

Education
The following education magazines have sometimes
included articles on computer graphics and computers
for presentation purposes.
American Educator (www.aeda.com)
American School Board Journal (www.asbj.com)
ASCD Education Update (www.ascd.org)
Center for Leadership and Technology (www.celt.org)
Education Week (www.edweek.org)

Popular Computing
These magazines, available at most bookstores and
newsstands, give overviews of new products, soft-
ware reviews, and some sort of question-and-answer
column. Though neither art- nor education-specific,
they often offer good insights, in simple terminology,
about the larger computer picture.
Byte (www.byte.com)
Family PC (www.familypc.com)
Home PC (www.homepc.com)
Mac Addict (www.macaddict.com)
Macworld (www.macworld.com)
PC Computing (www.pccomputing.com)
PC Today (www.pctoday.com)
PC World (www.pcworld.com)

The Internet
These magazines, available at large bookstores or
magazine stands, have many articles about the
Internet, reviews of Web sites, overviews and, in
some cases, ratings.
Internet World (www.internetworld.com)
Java Report (www.javareport.com)
Wired (www.wired.com)

Entertainment
Entertainment magazines (or their TV counterparts,
like E Network) often feature articles on the making
of a movie or TV show that incorporates special
effects or computer graphics.
Entertainment Magazine
Premier
Rolling Stone

Newspapers
Newspapers often have articles and/or columns dis-
cussing advances in technology that affect our lives.
The Los Angeles Times (www.latimes.com)
The New York Times (www.nytimes.com)

USA Today (www.usatoday.com)
Washington Post (www.washingtonpost.com)

Television

PBS has presented programs on computer graphics. *Nova, Innovation,* and *The Computer Chronicles* in particular have presented shows on computer technology. If your school district is a member of Public Broadcasting you may have permission to tape these programs for classroom use. The following channels have Web sites: MSNBC, CNN, PBS, Discovery, The Learning Channel, and A&E.

Organizations

SIGGRAPH Association for Computing Machinery
11 West 42nd Street, New York, NY 10036
(www.siggraph.org)
SIGGRAPH, begun in 1966 as a special-interest group on computer graphics, is an organization for graphic artists and fine artists to share information about using computers to create visual images. With a membership of over 12,000, SIGGRAPH sponsors an annual summer technical conference that includes full-day and half-day courses and tutorials, papers on the most recent advances in computer graphics, panels, and sigKIDS, which showcases innovative learning opportunities for children. The conference also features an art show of juried works created by the membership. (These works are available in 35-mm slide sets and videos.) In 1998, at the twenty-fifth annual conference, attendance at SIGGRAPH was over 30,000.

National Art Education Association
1916 Association Drive, Reston, Virginia 20191
(www.naea-reston.org)
For over fifty years, the National Art Education Association has been providing resources for art educators. Various periodicals (including art-education magazines) and books (including *New Technologies in Art Education: Implications for Theory, Research, and Practice*) offer information on technology, as well as practical applications for the art curriculum. In recent years, the annual conference has focused on technology, including hands-on computer labs and training workshops.

Your state's department of education may be another helpful resource. And don't forget your state art-education associations (for a listing of those with Web sites, see www.cedarnet.org/emig).

International Society for Technology Education (ISTE) (www.iste.org)
ISTE is dedicated to promoting appropriate uses of information technology to support and improve learning, teaching, and administration in K–12 education and teacher education. ISYE sponsors NECC, the National Educational Computing Conference.

Association for the Advancement of Computing in Education (AACE) (www.aace.org)
Geared to help teachers integrate technology into their classroom on a daily basis.

Association for Educational Communications and Technology (www.aect.org)
Provides leadership in educational communications and technology by linking professionals holding a common interest in the use of educational technology and its application to the learning process.

International Association of Computer Graphics (IACG) (www.iacgr.com)
The IACG promotes arts done in computer media. The Web site includes artist and gallery listings, news, events, and articles. Galleries and artists are encouraged to submit their work.

State Departments of Education will also be helpful. And, don't forget your State Art Education Associations!

Artists

The study of art is not limited to the study of technique and skill. A study of artists and their works is also part of art education. The list below is certainly not exhaustive, but may be of help in establishing a critical and aesthetic base for discussion of computer art as an art form. Consult your local museums and galleries for the names of additional artists. Colleges and universities may also prove a valuable resource. Some artists are: Charles Csuri, Stewart Dickson,* Susumu Endo,* Larry Elin, David Em, Darcy Gerbarg, Aldo Giorgini, Karen Huff, Kenneth Knowlton, Dorothy Krause,* Robert Mallary, Aaron Marcus, Leslie Mezei, Ann Murray, Eihachiro

Nakame, Barbara Nessim,* Melvin Prueitt, Joseph Scala, Patsy Scala, Lillian Schwartz, Steve Strassman, Peter Struycken, Joan Truckenbrod,* John Whitney.

* Represented by the Williams Gallery (www.wmgallery.com)

Museums

Museums exhibit both computer-generated artworks and installations and multimedia showcases that use computers in some way. In the past, smaller museums and galleries were at the forefront of exhibiting multimedia, computer, and video artworks.

New Resources

CD-ROMs

Although the number of CD-ROM titles has grown significantly in the past few years, those created specifically for art education are limited. Some are "catalogs" of artworks; others are wonderful adventures into the world of art and artist.

Because of legal and artistic considerations, the creating of comprehensive CD-ROMs in art has been difficult. Museums, mindful of their role as guardians of artworks, are hesitant to permit wide reproduction of any art image on disc. Many of the larger museums have created their own discs, or are cooperating with large software companies, and they have produced very well done interactive programs. Current trends show museums making their Web sites more comprehensive as they catalogue and publish exhibits on the Web.

CD-ROM technology is ideal for discipline-based art education (DBAE)—an approach that integrates art production with art history, criticism, and aesthetics. Not only does it provide accessibility to the art image, but also students and teachers can use authoring systems to develop resources. (For more information about using CD-ROM in your curriculum, see pages 21–25.)

In the following list of CD-ROM titles, I have commented on those I've used. In the last edition of *New Technologies in the Artroom*, I included the publishers of this software. I have not done that here. Rather, I suggest you explore distributors, online resources, educational materials catalogues, and museums and museum shops for these titles and others like them. (I have even found CDs in department stores!) Some of these may no longer be available.

The Ultimate Frank Lloyd Wright – Excellent
Art Gallery of Art of London – Good
History Through Art Collection (800 BC–1550 AD) (4 CDs)
History Through Art Collection (1545 AD–1900 AD) (4 CDs)
Art and Music series
With Open Eyes – Very good
Painters Painting – Very good
Comic Book Confidential – Very good
I Photograph to Remember – Very good
Van Gogh: Starry Night – Very good
A Passion for Art: The Barnes Foundation – Very good
The Mastery of Michelangelo
Le Louvre
150 Years of America's Smithsonian
Masterpieces of Japanese Painting
Robert Mapplethorpe: An Overview
Great Paintings: Renaissance / Impressionism
Ancient Egyptian Art: Brooklyn Museum
Leonardo – The Paintings
Vincent Van Gogh: Life and Works
Paul Cézanne: Masterpieces from the Musée d'Orsay
Great Artists: In Association with the National Gallery
Escher Interactive – Very good
MOBA: The Virtual Museum of Bad Art
Michelangelo: Queue / E.M.M.E.
The Renaissance of Florence
The Sistine Chapel: Before and After Restoration
The Great Museums of Europe
Leonardo the Inventor
ArtRageous!
The Renaissance
1000 Years of Russian Art: the State Russian Museum, St. Petersburg
Ideadisc – Excellent
Amazing Animation
Animator 3-D Starter Kit

Not Art-Specific Titles But Good for Use in Art Programs

American Poetry
500 Nations
Her Heritage
Ancient Lands
Encarta (or any encyclopedia)
History of the World
Time Traveler CD-ROM

CD-ROM Reviews

Art Gallery:The Collection of the National Gallery of London
(Macintosh, Windows)
Suggested retail: $54.95; academic version $39.95
This is not just a collection of the works from the National Gallery in London; what it provides is an opportunity to explore the collection of over 2000 paintings available at the National Gallery and to branch out in a number of areas.

The Table of Contents is divided into five areas:

- *Artists' Lives* includes not only a biography but thumbnail images of artworks, allowing you to click forward to a full sized painting. You may also cross-reference by time period, or click to a word or name found in the glossary. An audio feature pronounces the name of the artist.
- *Picture Types* allows you to select a category of painting. Numerous examples are included for reference.
- *Historical Atlas* with detailed maps and timeline allows exploration by period or place.
- *General Reference* provides hundreds of terms, names, and images from the collection, as well as a general reference of stories from mythology, the Bible, and lives of the saints which can help students understand a painting.
- *Guided Tours* are arranged thematically: Composition and Painting, Making Paintings, Paintings as Objects and Beneath the Varnish. Taking a tour of Paintings as Objects brings you to a narration discussing paintings used as objects; the first (of several) are altarpieces. The text includes information on the artist, composition and content of the altarpiece as well as an animation of the altarpiece closing revealing the paintings on the reverse sides. There are also highlighted words in the text. In the case of the Coronation of the Virgin by Giusto, these words include virgin, annunciate, shutter, and spandrels.

This disk can be used for demonstration purposes or as a point for discussion of an art history topic. The images are crisp and clear and there are several close ups and cartoons of images. Students can use it on their own to conduct research or to provide a context for further research. The disk is a good reference tool for library, classroom, or home use.

The Ultimate Frank Lloyd Wright: America's Architect
(Macintosh, Windows)
Suggested retail: $34.95; academic version $24.95
From the moment this CD launches, you are drawn into the world of Frank Lloyd Wright. Take an interactive 3-D walking tour of three of his structures; search his life and times in video, audio, and photography; or explore the elements and influences of his work. View buildings, windows, furnishings; big and small, finished and unfinished, interiors and exteriors. Included are images and landscapes that influenced his work, music and narration, even commentary from Wright himself. All of these are easily referenced and cross referenced.
The main menu offers the following:

- A *Walking Tour*: the Robie House, Larkin Building, and Ennis House; included is a model of each building and floor plans.
- His *Life and Times* (a chronology of Wright's life that includes video clips)
- *Wright Works* includes a look at the Chronology of Wright's Work, Wright's works around the United States, and Decorative Arts and Furnishings.
- *Structural Elements* The categories of philosophy, sites, patterns, materials, and types pertain to Wright's influences and philosophy. Illustrations and photography highlight these categories in his works.
- *Modeling Wright* provides an opportunity to design a house using Wright's Building Blocks.
- In the *Library*, one can search by topic or name for references.

Not all of this is perfect, and I hesitate to mention this at all but... as much as I loved the introduction, having to sit through it each time I wanted to launch the CD-ROM got very old, very fast; the interface isn't quite as friendly as others I've used (I had to read the accompanying instructions, although they were very brief) and Modeling Wright was only fair. Still, the overall look of this, from screen design to the variety of media used, to the content itself is *wonderful*. A great reference tool.

Teachers can make great use of this, even if architecture is not a strong focus. Wright is accessible and this disk is filled with images that bring his work to life; I found Structural Elements and the Life and

Times especially informative noting not only Wright's influence on architecture, but the variety of people, places, and things that inspired Wright. Students can use this to research, write a term paper, or have fun with the building blocks.

The History Through Art series
Clearvue Inc. & ZCI Publishing, Inc.
Set of 9 programs: *Ancient Greece Through the Twentieth Century*
(Macintosh, Windows, DOS)
Sold individually or as a set. Set of 9: $595.95; Individual: $74.95; Lab Packs: $224.95
Also available on videotape. Set of 9: $695.00; 84.95
(courtesy of Sax Arts and Crafts)
The History Through Art series from Clearvue that was done in the early 1990s on videotape is now on CD-ROM. *The Renaissance, The Pre-Modern Era,* and the *Twentieth Century* were quite good. If you have any of the videotapes, you'll be pleased to see what has been done on the CD-ROM. While the images and script are the same as on the videotapes, there is so much more.

These information-filled CD-ROMs present the various artworks in the historical, religious, and cultural context in which they were created. While Western painting is the mainstay of this series, there are sculptures, architecture, icons, and photographs as well. The interactivity is good for individual-student exploration.

Here are the good points.
- There is a multimedia feature presentation, which takes you through the disk.
- A dictionary, a limited encyclopedia, a glossary, and an index are included.
- At the bottom of screen, the script is visible, with highlighted words that link to the dictionary or encyclopedia (green = dictionary; blue = encyclopedia).
- Names of artist and titles of works are on-screen.
- You can bring images to full screen.
- Through the index, you can reach any other part of the CD-ROM.
- Through a search, you can go to particular slides or pages.
- Music is included.
- Questions and quizzes with immediate feedback
Here are the not-so-good points.
- No documentation is included. There should be

a printed list of images, study questions, and/or guidelines for teachers that address each specific disk.
- The color reproduction for some images is poor.
- The cost might be beyond some budgets.

Splendors of Imperial China: Treasures from the National Palace Museum, Taipei: The Metropolitan Museum of Art
(Macintosh, Windows)
More than 475 paintings, calligraphy, carved objects, and porcelain pieces from the National Palace Museum, Taipei are presented on this CD-ROM. Originally designed to be viewed as part of the museum experience, this CD has no audio commentary; what it does have is a rich collection of support material (including translations and biographies) to assist the viewer through the "tour." Some might find the absence of a commentary a bit disturbing, but when you realize it was meant to be viewed as part of the exhibition, the reason for the silence is obvious

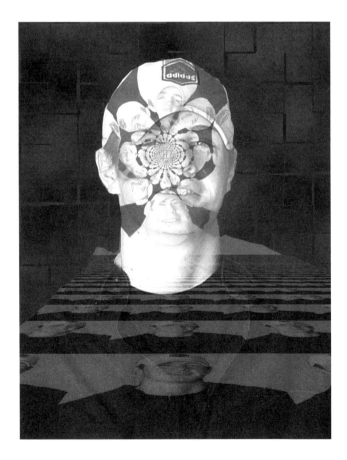

Mike Moore
Untitled, *Photoshop*
Randolph High School, Morristown, NJ

(and besides, if your students use this in class, you may welcome the relative quiet!). The images are logically presented with a table of contents dividing images into periods; maps and a timeline are also available. This is a wonderful opportunity for students to explore some of the richness of the arts of China, an area often given limited study. (Note: a friend who has seen these pieces in Taipei thought the images were well displayed here.)

Van Gogh: Starry Night
Voyager, distributed by Forest Technologies
This is *not* a collection of all of van Gogh's works (the number of images is limited), nor is it a typical look at the artist's work. What it is, however, is an exploration of van Gogh as an intelligent, practical man influenced by the events and discoveries of his time. His paintings are viewed not as the markings of a man mentally imbalanced, but of an intelligent, thoughtful explorer searching for answers.

This CD-ROM is driven by the work of author Al Boime, who narrates a serious look at *Starry Night*. The disc also contains Boime's "A History of Matter, A Matter of History," a series of letters from van Gogh written in 1889 and 1890, a glossary, and an index of the images.

Boime's in-depth look at *Starry Night* goes beyond the commercialism that has made the artwork a cliché. Boime discusses the influences of science, astronomy (and the work of astronomer Camille Flammarion), science fiction (Jules Verne), religion, and the events of van Gogh's time (the exposition of Paris of 1889 and the Eiffel Tower) on his work.

This is a wonderful disc for students to explore fully the work of this great artist and the depth and variety of events, discoveries, and personal interests that influenced his work.

A Passion for Art: The Barnes Foundation
Corbis Publishing, 1995
(written with Daphne Williams, Teachers College student) See page 24 for a complete description.

Videodiscs

Believe it or not, I was recently given five videodiscs! My school still has a videodisc player, and if you can figure out how to connect it to a pro-

jector, it can be used just like a CD-ROM. Videodiscs are no longer being produced, but I've included these in case you find a player in your school. You could search these titles on e-bay!
Andrew Wyeth: The Helga Pictures
Dream Machine (Parts 1, 2, and 3)
The Greek Vases
The Louvre
The National Gallery of Art Videodisc
Persistence of Vision
Philip Pearlstein Draws the Artist's Model
Profiles in American Art
Vincent van Gogh: A Portrait in Two Parts

Like CD-ROMs, these discs attend to a variety of learning situations. For example, one side of the van Gogh disc presents a guided tour through the various periods of his life and work, and is interspersed with single still frames of his work. The other side is a dramatization of van Gogh's life as seen through the eyes of his brother Theo.

The National Gallery videodisc presents a tour of the gallery on one side, and over 15,000 frames of artwork on the other. After students take a tour through the National Gallery, or see a vignette or short segment about a particular period in art history, you could ask questions that attend to the goals of DBAE. You could then ask about a particular style or period, or an aspect of art criticism or aesthetics.

Web Sites

There are hundreds of art-related Web sites. I have listed some of the more interesting ones and those that have many links to get you to other resources. This is by no means an exhaustive list! Go to any search engine and investigate their arts and entertainment sections for many more sites.

Note: This is a partial listing. Unfortunately, Web sites come and go. You might find a great site one day, and return another day to find it has been taken over by someone else. The sites included in this list tend to be well-maintained.

Art Education Sites
www.artsonia.com/
Focused on integrating art, technology, and education; includes a teacher section, student section, and thematic section, also lesson plans and project ideas. It is a wonderful place to display student work.

www.artteacherconnection.com/pages/home.htm
Lesson plans/project ideas integrating art and technology, links to museums, art standards, software recommendations, and evaluations/assessments.

arttech.about.com
This site has several good links and is informative.

artsedge.kennedy-center.org/
Curricular information, and an ideas exchange. Layout is easy and straightforward.

www.artsednet.getty.edu/
From the Getty Institute for the Arts, features lesson plans and curricular ideas, image galleries, and links.

www.kinderart.com/lessons.htm
Lessons for elementary using art for topics such as the underground railroad, art book projects, printmaking, etc.

www.vue.org
Explains and explores Visual Thinking Strategy (VTS) — teaching children the skill of observation builds their visual acuity, improves their powers of observation, and moves the students through Abigail Housen's stage theory.

www.crayola.com
Some fun categories are activity book, card creator, inspiring ideas, media center, and more. It also offers many lesson sources and ideas on specific topic. It has separate sections for parents, educators and children to search according to their needs.

Tools and Tutorials
www.webmonkey.com
Web Developers Resources offers tutorials and FAQs for beginners, builders, masters and even kids! Great ideas and lessons for children; great answers to questions and tutorials for you!

www.colormatters.com/
Just about everything you wanted to know about colors starting with basic color theory. There is also an informative section about computers and color, which includes a color blind test for your computer.

www.graphic-design.com/Photoshop/
Several graphic artists offer tips on using Photoshop.

www.rpi.edu/~huntea/computer_art/COLORlab.html
Information on the color wheel and matching colors.

www.flamingtext.com
On this site you are able to create headings in all different types of fonts, colors, and sizes and then save them to use in any document. Also: clipart and buttons.

www.newentrepreneur.com/
Robert C. Parker has written books such as *Looking Good in Print*. He was among the first to publish books aimed at the desktop publisher who had no formal training in graphic design. Tips and worksheets for desktop publishing, Web design, and effective presentations.

www.urlsinternetcafe.com/classroom/features/index.html
Robin Williams was also among the first to address desktop publishing for those without a design background. This site has tips on fashioning a web page and using Adobe PageMaker 6.5 (Mac or PC).

www.Adobe.com
Information and FAQs from the makers of Photoshop!

General Educational Resources
www.scholastic.com
This popular site is divided into three sections: families, kids, and teachers. The teacher section offers many creative lesson ideas. Teachers can search by grade levels.

sunsite.berkeley.edu/KidsClick!
offers many interesting topics for children to search through. Teachers can also search for lesson ideas or visual aids.

www.howstuffworks.com
This site, as its name implies, is all about explaining how stuff works. It's a great resource to satisfy curious minds.

www.classroom.com/community/connection
Part of a larger site related to the Classroom Connect project; fabulous articles and links to lesson plans, teacher chat rooms, and links.

www.discoveryschool.com
A great website for teachers in any field. Features include the puzzle maker, quiz center, worksheet generator, etc. Educational links and games to challenge students, parents, and teachers.

www.eduweb.com/adventure.html
On-line activities and games bring various topics to life. Subject areas include science, social studies, art, and geography.

www.quia.com/
This is great if you are in search of templates to create on-line activities and games. They have templates for: concentration, matchings, word searches, quizzes, hangman, scavenger hunt, rags to riches activities, etc.

wwww.iwebquest.com/
Created by a former educator, about how to create a webquest. Step by step process, plus webquest links and treasure hunts.

www.ed.gov/technology
Government viewpoints on issues related to technology in education.

www.lightspan.com
A myriad of resources for teachers, parents, and kids. Internet projects, lesson plans, games for kids, virtual field trips, and so on.

www.education-world.com
A good site to find information on any teaching-related topic. Chat rooms, articles, lesson plans, information on how to publish a book, and so on.

www.discovery.com/exp/fossilzone/fossilzone.html
I wish I had found this site during the year. You can hear sounds of dinosaurs, look at pictures, play a survival game, and create a dinosaur.

http://marcopolo.worldcom.com
MarcoPolo
This site has two categories: teacher-supportive links and links to national councils for different subjects; the lesson plans are very interesting.

www.pbs.org
There are several sites on pbs.org that art teachers will love exploring! You can go to pbs.org and "explore by subject" and select "arts and culture." From there you can explore a variety of topics. Here are a few you won't want to miss:
www.pbs.org/art21/
www.pbs.org/wnet/americanmasters/
www.pbs.org/wnet/egg/index_flash.html
www.pbs.org/wnet/aaworld/arts/
www.pbs.org/wgbh/cultureshock/
www.pbskids.org

www.cnn.com
The education component of this news site provides teachers with articles written for and/or by students in a variety of subjects. It also has games and great resources.

www.apple.com/education
Yes, this site promotes Apple's products, but there are also a number of resources and stories of classroom teachers using a variety of technology in their classroom.

Museums and More
www.artmuseumnetwork.org
Art Museum Network
The world's largest and most prestigious art museums have joined forces to provide free access to information about their collections, exhibitions, and services.

www.icom.org/vlmp
Virtual Library Museum
It is often difficult and expensive to find replications of famous pieces of art. This site allows you to visit the museums where the art is housed and show your students the original pieces of art. Most museums supply accompanying information.

www.louvre.fr/louvrea.htm
The Louvre
One of the most extensive art collections in the world!

www.metmuseum.org
Metropolitan Museum of Art
The Metropolitan Museum of Art's site now offers a timeline along with a variety of resources for families and educators.

www.philamuseum.org
Philadelphia Museum of Arts
This site offers information for teachers and parents. It also offers distance learning so schools can use the museum to teach art education using video systems. Although the collections shown are limited, a variety of collections from different regions are presented.

www.nma.org
National Museum of Art
Each link is filled with all sorts of goodies that are representative of diverse cultural and educational content. Check out the links that feature artists and their notable works. The content is integrated into concise lesson plans.

www.amnh.org
American Museum of Natural History
This site also links to the Hayden Planetarium.

www.sfmoma.org/msoma/index.html
"Making Sense of Modern Art" is worth a look. I like the opportunity to compare different works of art next to each other.

www.moma.org
Museum of Modern Art
Check out the Art Safari in the Educational Resources section of this site. Students go on a safari to explore art—they are guided to become the interpreters of the artwork.

www.Whitney.org
The Whitney Museum
Explore the Whitney's collection of American art.

www.guggenheim.org
Guggenheim Museum
Explore the collections and the education programs.

www.walkerart.org
The Walker Art Museum
I picked this site initially because it is part of Artsconnected—www.artsconnected.org—a website for art education created by a consortium of Minnesota art museums that has been doing some really creative work.

www.ammi.org/site/site.asp
American Museum of the Moving Image
This museum is dedicated to educating the public about the art, history, technique, and technology of film, television, and digital media, and to examining their impact on culture and society. It maintains the nation's largest permanent collection of moving image artifacts.

www.mediaandtechnology.org
The American Association of museums, Media and Technology Committee sponsors this site. Don't miss the MUSE Awards section, showing "excellence in all varieties of media programs produced by or for museums."

sln.fi.edu
Benjamin Franklin Institute of Science and Technology
This site provides general information and special events.

www.lsc.org
Liberty Science Center, New Jersey

www.si.edu
Smithsonian Institute

www.artchive.com
Mark Harden's Artchive
The site includes: The Artchive, Glyphs Art Reviews, link to art exhibit reviews, Theory and Criticism, Art CD-ROM Reviews, and Art Links. The links are divided into Museums, Artists, and Resources.

www.artcyclopedia.com
The Fine Arts Search Engine! This is a great resource for researching by artists. An interesting feature allows you to find artist by art-history movement. The site also includes links to museums where the artist's work can be found.

www.amico.org
Art Museum Image Consortium
AMICO is a not-for-profit organization of institutions with collections of art, collaborating to enable educational use of museum multimedia. The AMICO Library™ is a licensed digital educational resource available under subscription to universities and colleges, public libraries, elementary and secondary schools, and museums.

Looking for Digital Artists?
www.iadas.net
Presented by The International Academy of Digital Arts and Sciences, The Webby Awards is the leading international honor for achievement in technology and creativity. Learn more by viewing the winners at www.webbyawards.com/main.

More and more artists are creating their own web sites. The following sites include organizations that support artists using technology and will lead you to a number of digital artists and their works:

www.digitalartsource.com
Digital Art Source is a resource for digital art and culture information.

www.siggraph.org
ACM SIGGRAPH is dedicated to the generation and dissemination of information on computer graphics and interactive techniques.

www.the-ada.com
The Alliance of Digital Artists
The mission statement notes: "Whilst there are specific organizations that cater for designers, illustrators and other areas of design, there is currently nothing available to address the unique requirements for those individuals involved in using technology to produce digital graphics and art in all of its many and varied applications."

home.earthlink.net/~havencars/iada
The International Association of Digital Artists (IADA) was established by and for digital artists, to significantly support and advance the marketability of both fine and commercial digital art.

www.wmgallery.com
For forty years the Williams Gallery has been supporting, representing, and showcasing computer artists.

www.thedigitalartist.com
View works by emerging and established artists, read articles on the business of art, find books on art, design and crafts.

www.art.net/studios/digital.html
Arts on the Net is an art gallery on the net! Features a gallery of digital art.

www.wwar.com
Site with links to hundreds of galleries, on-line exhibits and artists. Great database to search for artists, contemporary and historical.

Media Related
A number of media-related sites have interesting content (the latest in film, TV, recording industry, and so on) and have given their considerable creative and monetary support to the development of these web pages. They feature sound, movie clips, animation and even some opportunity for interactivity. Take a look at the design, even if you are not interested in the content.

Television:
www.abc.com
www.nbc.com
www.cbs.com
www.cnn.com
www.foxnet.com
www.pbs.org
www.scifi.com
www.msnbc.com
www.discovery.com
www.aetv.com
www.mtv.com
www.bravotv.com
www.ovationtv.com

Film studios and big conglomerates:
www.lucasarts.com
www.disney.com
www.mca.com
www.warnerbros.com
www.sony.com (films and music)

www.ifilms.com (new and independent films)
www.atom films.com (independent films and animation
www.pixar.com
www.aardman.com

Advertising agencies and public relations firms:
www.adage.com
www.ogilvy.com
www.jwtworld.com

Nontraditional Resources

- Business (such as quick-copy or offset printers)
  Local businesses are often willing to help out a
  local school. Certainly, no printer can print out
  every image your students create, but perhaps
  you could run a contest in your school or district and the top five winners would get their
  image printed out by a professional printer. You
  might also talk with local printers about printing supplies, particularly special papers.
- Industry
  While you may not want old computers, what
  about old printers or scanners or editing equipment? Your equipment doesn't have to be new, it
  just needs to work. Older computers are slower
  and may not have the memory you want . . . but
  they're better than nothing. Take whatever you
  can get, as long as it works.
- Cable Providers and Channel One
  When the franchises for operation were negotiated several years ago, most communities
  included access to video production and distribution. In some cases, this means TV equipment
  for community use and a cable community-
  access channel.

  Many schools use Chris Whittles' Channel
  One or their local cable channel for access to
  CNN, or use some other news outlet and have
  at their disposal a good deal of video equipment. You might be able to use the equipment
  in your classroom.

IMAGE FILE FORMAT TERMS

GIF	graphics interchange format
JPEG	joint photographic expert group. You may have to zip (compress) your image files so that they fit on a Web page. Because a JPEG file is about one-fourth the size of a corresponding GIF file, zipping is usually not necessary.
QuickTime	video file format
MPEG	motion picture experts group (a compression standard)
MPEG2	motion picture experts group (updated version of MPEG)
JAVA	computer language used for delivering application programs over the Internet
EPS	encapsulated postscript
PCX	Windows format used by paint programs
PICT	Mac format used by paint programs
BMP	bitmap file (Windows)
TIFF	tagged image file format
TARGA	now JPEG
AVI	movie clips; audio-visual

GLOSSARY

access: retrieval of information from a storage medium (such as a computer disk, optical disc, or tape).

aliasing: in computer-generated images, a stepped edge or "staircase" that appears along lines not perfectly horizontal or vertical.

analog: describing information that flows or changes. Analog devices are characterized by dials and/or sliding mechanisms.

animation: the process of giving motion to an image.

antialiasing: a technique used to smooth out jagged edges that appear around text and graphics on-screen. *See also* aliasing.

artificial intelligence: (AI) the capability of a machine to perform functions usually associated with human intelligence, such as learning and adapting to change.

authoring system: software (e.g., HyperStudio) that allows nonprogrammers to use the computer to design programs or interactive courseware.

AVI: (audio-visual interface) an extension that refers to audio-video files.

baud: a unit of speed for transmission of data: usually associated with modems.

binary: referring to the representation of data in terms of the two ("bi-") digits 0 and 1.

bit: the smallest unit of information storage on computers.

BMP: an extension that refers to a paint file (or bitmap) in Windows.

browser: a program (e.g., Netscape, Explorer) that allows users to access the Web.

brush: in graphics software, a defined point used as a cursor, to create strokes of various widths and sizes on the monitor.

byte: a unit of information composed of consecutive bits, usually 8 or 16. One byte is treated as a unit by a computer.

CAD/CAM: (computer-aided design/computer-aided manufacturing) a wide range of systems that assist mechanical, architectural, or electronic drawing.

camcorder: a device that contains both a video camera and a videocassette recorder.

cartridge: a removable storage device (tape or disk). Also refers to what holds the ink supply for an ink-jet printer.

CD: (compact disc) a 4 3/4" disc used to store audio or visual images in digital form. This format is usually associated with audio information.

CD-R: (compact discs–recordable) a storage disc that allows users with a special drive to record onto it.

CD-ROM: (compact disc–read-only memory) a 4 3/4" laser-encoded optical storage disc. The information on these discs cannot be altered.

CD-RW: (compact disk–rewritable) a storage disc that allows users with a special drive to rewrite a CD.

chip: a wafer of silicon containing thousands of integrated circuits.

command: a communication from the user to the computer, which directs the computer to execute specific instructions.

compression: the process, usually done with compression software, by which a computer file is reduced to create more disk space.

computer language: a method of instructing a computer, or a set of commands for programming a computer to perform a specific task. Some languages are C++, BASIC, and JAVA.

CPU: (central processing unit) the heart of the computer system, which performs the actual processing of information.

CRT: (cathode ray tube) a TV-like screen that displays information. Also called a monitor.

cursor: a small marker or symbol displayed on-screen and used to position text; in drawing programs, the current on-screen position of a selected menu command.

data: information prepared for input or output by a computer.

desktop publishing: the design and production (text formatting, creation of page layouts or composition, use of graphics) for publications, using a microcomputer.

desktop video: using the computer and appropriate software to create and/or edit video information.

digital: expressed in digits. Computers process digital information in 0s and 1s.

digital camera: a camera that allows users to take pictures on disc. The camera either saves direct-to-disc, or images are transferred via cable to computer.

digitize: to put analog information into digital form.

digitizer: a device that transforms analog information into digital information.

disk: *See* floppy disk, hard disk.

disk drive: *See* drive.

display: the visible picture on the screen or monitor. Also the screen itself.

documentation: the instruction manual that accompanies a software package, input device, or hardware.

dot-matrix printer: a printer that creates characters (letters/numbers) or graphics from a two-dimensional array of dots. The resulting characters and graphics consist of small dots.

download: to transfer files to one computer from another via a modem.

drive: a device that reads and writes data, and then puts it onto a storage medium, such as a diskette.

DVD: (digital versatile disc) the size of a CD, a two-sided disc that holds 4.7 GB of information per layer, enough for a 133-minute movie. With two layers on each side, it can hold up to 17 GB of information. A DVD-ROM player can also play CD-ROMs.

DVI: (digital-video interactive) a compact disc and a driver that allow for visual, audio, and text information, and also full-motion video.

edit: to change all or part of an image or text.

e-mail: documents or messages sent or received electronically through a telecommunications link.

EPS: (encapsulated PostScript) an extension that refers to images and graphics meant to be sent to a printer, and generally not meant for multimedia.

error message: an on-screen notification that tells the user that there is a problem in the execution of a command.

expansion card: a card inside the CPU that allows users to add extra capabilities to the computer.

expansion slot: a slot inside the CPU that holds the expansion card.

fax: (facsimile) an image or text transmitted over telephone lines.

fiber optics: the technology of transmitting information through plastic or glass fibers.

file: a collection of related data (text or graphics) stored on disk.

floppy disk: originally, a 5 1/4" flexible platter coated with magnetic material, used to store information. The newer 3 1/2" disks, called floppies or diskettes, are in a plastic casing, as are Zip disks.

font: a set of characters and symbols, such as an alphabet, in a particular size and style.

format: to prepare a blank disk to receive information. *See also* initialize.

FTP: (file-transfer protocol) a set of rules for the transfer of data, which allows files to be exchanged between different computers, usually via the Internet.

GB: (gigabyte) a unit of information equal to one billion bytes.

GIF: (graphic-interchange format) an extension that refers to compressed graphics files, which are limited in color and found on on-line services and the Internet.

graphics tablet: an input device, also called a digitizer tablet, that is an electronic board. The user draws on the board, which causes the cursor to move across the monitor in an equivalent position.

GUI: (graphical user interface) an extension with menus and icons that allows users to control the computer without using lines of computer code.

hard copy: a printed or plotted copy of the computer's output (text or graphics).

hard disk: an inflexible magnetic disk with greater storage capacity and faster access than a floppy, or diskette.

hardware: the physical equipment of a computer system, including the keyboard, CPU, monitor, and printer.

HDTV: (high-definition television) digital television with better resolution and a wider screen than we presently have.

HTML: (hypertext markup language) the hypertext language associated with Web pages. See also hypertext.

HyperCard: Apple software for the Macintosh that allows the user to create and link multiple sources of information.

hypermedia: a way to create and access large multimedia information sources or databases; usually includes the interaction of videodisc and hypercard stacks.

Hypertalk: the authoring language of HyperCard.

hypertext: an approach to information management of not only text, but also video and audio.

icon: an on-screen image or symbol that represents a command, function, document, or application.

initialize: to prepare a blank diskette to store information. *See also* format.

ink-jet printer: a nonimpact printer. A small series of ink-filled cartridges spray ink on the paper.

input device: an instrument—such as a joystick, light pen, tablet, or mouse—that allows users to give instructions or data to the computer.

integrated software: a package such as ClarisWorks and Microsoft Office that integrates several different programs into one system. The programs work together and can share data.

interactive: describing the participation of a user in directing the course of a program. A system that exchanges information with the user.

interface: an electronic link between computer components that allows one component to communicate with another.

the Internet: a worldwide network of networks offering the World Wide Web, e-mail, newsgroups, and so on.

I/O: (input/output) an input device such as the joystick or mouse, or an output device such as a printer.

ISP: (Internet service provider) an online Internet provider.

Java: a programming language designed for use in the Internet, it can be used to create complete applications or to build small application modules for use as part of a Web page.

joystick: a leverlike input device mounted in a small box. When the lever is swiveled or rotated from the central point, the cursor follows that action on-screen.

JPEG: (Joint Photographic Experts Group) a format that compresses an image.

K: the abbreviation for kilo ("one thousand"), it describes the memory of a computer, such as 16K, 48K, 64K, 128K.

keyboard: an input device with alpha-numeric keys by which users type information into the computer.

laser: usually refers to a specific kind of light beam.

laser printer: a printer whose output, either graphics or text, is created by a laser beam that traces the image onto paper with toner.

LCD panel: (liquid crystal display) about the size of a laptop computer, a panel used with an overhead projector to project an image from computer and/or video to wall or screen.

letter-quality printer: an impact printer that produces documents in much the same way as a typewriter.

light pen: an electronic pen connected to the computer. It allows users to "draw" on-screen. As the pen touches the screen, the cursor appears and follows the movement of the pen.

load: to transfer a file or graphics image from disk to main memory. *See also* download.

MB: (megabyte) a storage-capacity unit used to describe the memory of a CPU (e.g., 16 MB of RAM) or the storage capacity of a removable disc or diskette.

memory: the main internal storage area of a computer where instructions for an in-use program are temporarily kept.

menu: a displayed list of options from which users select an action to be performed.

MHz: (megahertz) a measure for the speed of the computer processor.

MIDI: (musical instrument digital interface) a computer system that creates, records, and plays back electronic music.

mirror: a menu option that allows users to have strokes made on one section of the screen mirrored exactly on the opposing half, or a selected section of the screen.

modem: a device that enables the computer to transmit and receive information over a telephone line.

monitor: the computer screen.

mouse: a small, boxlike input device with a roller ball on the underside. As the user moves the mouse across a flat surface, the cursor moves across the screen.

MPEG: (Moving Picture Experts Group) established to develop standards for moving pictures, audio, and their combination, this group is involved in developing standards for digital, video, and audio compression.

network: a group of communication lines that link various computers for sharing of information.

NTSC: (National Television Systems Committee) in the U.S., the current NTSC format is 525-line scan lines with a frame frequency of 1/30 of a second.

output: information transferred by the computer to an external device such as the screen, printer, or plotter.

page: an area of memory sufficient to hold one full screen of information.

paint program: a software package that allows users to draw freehand directly into the computer, with an input device.

palette: a selection of colors available in a graphics display system.

peripheral: a device that is external to the computer itself, such as a printer, an input device, or a modem.

PICT: a Macintosh file format for moving graphics files between various programs.

pixel (picture element): a video image-forming unit. The more pixels per screen, the finer the images that can be drawn. *See also* resolution.

plotter: an output device, used mainly by engineers and architects, that records lines, letters, and graphics symbols.

presentation graphics: graphics, such as business charts and graphs, designed to present information.

printout: a hard copy of information in a file or some section of memory.

QuickTime: Apple's architecture for working with time-based data (sounds and video). It allows users to play digital movies and video, making multimedia on computers possible.

QuickTime VR: part of QuickTime, QuickTime VR (virtual reality) allows users to create a virtual room, building, or environment (both interiors and exteriors) by shooting a series of still pictures in complete circles from various points in relation to the object or environment desired. It "merges" the still pictures to create the virtual world.

RAM (random access memory): memory where information can be easily written or retrieved; often refers to comuter memory (16M RAM, 32M RAM).

rendering: a process in which a computer calculates the final version of a 3-D wire-frame model, drawing the surfaces, textures, and/or lighting selected by the artist or designer.

resolution: the detail of a display screen, as defined by the number of pixels the screen is capable of displaying. The higher the resolution, the finer the detail of the image.

RF modulator: a device that converts computer signals to signals that can be displayed on a TV screen.

RGB: (red, green, blue) describes a color display or monitor.

ROM (read-only memory): Storage that can be read from, but not written to; often refers to a CD-ROM.

rubber banding: a technique for forming some shapes. To make a rectangle, the user anchors the cursor in a position and then drags, or "rubber bands," the opposing corner of the rectangle until it reaches the desired size.

scan: to analyze data.

scanner: a device that turns an image into digital form for input into the computer.

sector: a portion of the recording surface of any disk.

stack: a group of cards (information displayed on-screen) created through HyperCard.

TIFF: (tagged image file format) one of the most popular graphics formats for photographs.

track: a portion of a disk consisting of circles or bands, for storing data.

trackball: a type of mouse that users control by rolling a stationary ball.

tutorial: a software program that gives instruction.

utility: a program that performs specialized tasks.

VGA (video graphics array): a monitor offered by IBM and clones, with a resolution of 640 x 480 (pixels).

videodisc: a storage medium for visual images.

window: a defined area of the display screen that can be used independently of other areas.

workstation: a configuration of computer equipment. A graphics workstation includes the computer and at least one input device, color monitor, and output device.

INDEX